CW01065229

Tower Vortx Digital Air Fryer Oven Cookbook UK 2023

1000 Days Easy & Delicious Tower Air Fryer Recipes for Beginners to have Fun Cooking and Eating

Gloria Simpkins

All Rights Reserved.

The content contained within this book may not be reproduced, duplicated, or transmitted without direct written permission from the author or the publisher. Under no circumstances will any blame or legal responsibility be held against the publisher, or author, for any damages, reparation, or monetary loss due to the information contained within this book, either directly or indirectly.

Legal Notice: This book is copyright protected. It is only for personal use. You cannot amend, distribute, sell, use, quote or paraphrase any part, or the content within this book, without the consent of the author or publisher.

Disclaimer Notice:

Please note the information contained within this document is for educational and entertainment purposes only. All effort has been executed to present accurate, up to date, reliable, complete information. No warranties of any kind are declared or implied. Readers acknowledge that the author is not engaged in the rendering of legal, financial, medical, or professional advice. The content within this book has been derived from various sources. Please consult a licensed professional before attempting any techniques outlined in this book. By reading this document, the reader agrees that under no circumstances is the author responsible for any losses, direct or indirect, that are incurred as a result of the use of the information contained within this document, including, but not limited to, errors, omissions, or inaccuracies.

CONTENTS

Beef & Lamb And Pork Recipes 35

Poultry Recipes 47

Introduction

Why Air Frying?

Air frying is increasingly popular because it allows you to quickly and evenly prepare delicious meals with little fat and little effort. Here are just a few of the reasons you'll want to switch to air frying:

It replaces other cooking appliances. You can use the air fryer in place of your oven, microwave, deep fryer, and dehydrator. Using one small device, you can quickly cook perfect dishes for every meal without sacrificing flavor.

It cooks faster than traditional cooking methods. Air frying works by circulating hot air around the cooking chamber. This results in fast and even cooking, using a fraction of the energy of your oven. Most air fryers can be set to a maximum temperature of 400°F, so just about anything you can make in an oven, you can make in an air fryer.

It uses little to no cooking oil. A main selling point of air fryers is that you can achieve beautifully cooked foods using little to no cooking oil. Whether you're following a diet or not, you can probably appreciate lower fat and calorie content. The air fryer helps make that possible.

Cleanup is fast. Any method of cooking will dirty your cooker, but your air fryer's smaller cooking chamber and removable basket make thorough cleanup a breeze!

What a Towe Air Fryer Oven is

The Towe brand was founded in the 1970s. Its founders (The Sontheimer) visited a home goods fair in France. This fateful journey led to the introduction of the American food processor, which was modeled on a similar device that the French called a robotic coupe. For many years after that, Towe only made kitchen machines. Towe did not develop further until the 1990s and offered other items to make life in the kitchen easier. The name Towe has stood for quality, innovative products, and design for many years.

The Towe Air Fryer Oven is the newest addition to the line of innovative kitchen appliances of Towe. It serves as an air fryer and a fast and efficient electric oven, and a toaster. It is an electric air fryer that has rapid airflow technology. This appliance is perfect for people who love to cook crispy food in a large amount. The Towe Air Fryer is readily available on its online stores and Amazon, and this countertop convection oven comes with accessories including Towe air fryer, baking pan and air fry basket. It boasts the following features:

1800-watt motor, fan, and heater.

Wide temperature range: 80°F to 450°F.

Selecting presets, temperature, time, and function has never been easier with an extensive digital display and intuitive programming options.

Adaptable Thermostat, 60 Minutes Auto shut off, Selector-Timer of Toast Shade Internally.

A range of 7 functions: Air fry, Convection bake, Convection broil, Bake, Broil, Warm & Toast

Easy cleanup: nonstick interior, dishwasher-safe Baking Tray, Oven Rack, Air Fryer Basket, Whisper for Quiet Operation

Advantages of the Towe Air Fryer Oven

1.When you are cooking for a family, you need a device that has a larger capacity—the Towe is the device for you. It is larger than your standard air fryer or toaster oven without taking up too much extra space on your countertop. You will easily be able to cook meals that are meant to be eaten by multiple people without having to put in a lot of extra time or effort.

2.Because this device is multi-functional, it eliminates the need for you to have a separate air fryer and toaster oven. It is a 2-in-1 that will end up saving you money. Even if your budget isn't tight, it makes sense to save as much money as possible with the rising costs of food and other appliances like this on the market.

3.Nothing is worse than a cluttered countertop. It can become cumbersome when you have too many appliances to choose from. When you want to fry, bake, toast, or broil, you won't have to get out any additional appliances from your cupboards. The Towe fits neatly on your kitchen countertop, and it still leaves plenty of room for the rest of your appliances and kitchen items.

4.When you are cooking in large batches, one big problem that you encounter is unevenness in the final result. Even putting a large batch of veggies in the oven might result in some being well done while other pieces are undercooked. The air fryer element of the Towe eliminates this problem for you. With this device, you get even cooking every time. There is also no need to flip anything or adjust anything—all you need to do is put your ingredients inside and set the dials; it doesn't get any easier than this.

You are going to become a more efficient cook when you use your Towe. Because you do not have to constantly stand around to monitor if your food is going to burn or overcook, you can go about your day without any worries. It is a controlled method for cooking that offers you great results every time.

Cleaning Your Air Fryer

Before cleaning it, first ensure that your air fryer is completely cool and unplugged. To clean the air fryer pan you'll need to:

Remove the air fryer pan from the base. Fill the pan with hot water and dish soap. Let the pan soak with the frying basket inside for 10 minutes.

Clean the basket thoroughly with a sponge or brush.

Remove the fryer basket and scrub the underside and outside walls.

Clean the air fryer pan with a sponge or brush.

Let everything air-dry and return to the air fryer base.

To clean the outside of your air fryer, simply wipe with a damp cloth. Then, be sure all components are in the correct position before beginning your next cooking adventure.

Breakfast & Snacks And Fries Recipes

European Pancakes

Servings: 5
Cooking Time:xx
Ingredients:

- 3 large eggs
- 130g flour
- 140ml whole milk
- 2 tbsp unsweetened apple sauce
- A pinch of salt

Directions:

1. Set your fryer to 200ºC and add five ramekins inside to heat up
2. Place all your ingredients inside a blender to combine
3. Spray the ramekins with a little cooking spray
4. Pour the batter into the ramekins carefully
5. Fry for between 6-8 minutes, depending on your preference
6. Serve with your favourite toppings

Bocconcini Balls

Servings: 2
Cooking Time:xx
Ingredients:

- 70 g/½ cup plus ½ tablespoon plain/all-purpose flour (gluten-free if you wish)
- 1 egg, beaten
- 70 g/1 cup dried breadcrumbs (gluten-free if you wish; see page 9)
- 10 bocconcini

Directions:

1. Preheat the air-fryer to 200ºC/400ºF.
2. Place the flour, egg and breadcrumbs on 3 separate plates. Dip each bocconcini ball first in the flour to coat, then the egg, shaking off any excess before rolling in the breadcrumbs.
3. Add the breaded bocconcini to the preheated air-fryer and air-fry for 5 minutes (no need to turn them during cooking). Serve immediately.

French Toast Slices

Servings: 1
Cooking Time:xx
Ingredients:

- 2 eggs
- 5 slices sandwich bread

- 100ml milk
- 2 tbsp flour
- 3 tbsp sugar
- 1 tsp ground cinnamon
- 1/2 tsp vanilla extract
- Pinch of salt

Directions:

1. Preheat your air fryer to 220ºC
2. Take your bread and cut it into three pieces of the same size
3. Take a mixing bowl and combine the other ingredients until smooth
4. Dip the bread into the mixture, coating evenly
5. Take a piece of parchment paper and lay it inside the air fryer
6. Arrange the bread on the parchment paper in one layer
7. Cook for 5 minutes
8. Turn and cook for another 5 minutes

Oozing Baked Eggs

Servings: 2
Cooking Time:xx
Ingredients:

- 4 eggs
- 140g smoked gouda cheese, cut into small pieces
- Salt and pepper to taste

Directions:

1. You will need two ramekin dishes and spray each one before using
2. Crack two eggs into each ramekin dish
3. Add half of the Gouda cheese to each dish
4. Season and place into the air fryer
5. Cook at 350ºC for 15 minutes, until the eggs are cooked as you like them

Wholegrain Pitta Chips

Servings: 2
Cooking Time:xx
Ingredients:

- 2 round wholegrain pittas, chopped into quarters
- 1 teaspoon olive oil
- ½ teaspoon garlic salt

Directions:

1. Preheat the air-fryer to 180ºC/350ºF.
2. Spray or brush each pitta quarter with olive oil and sprinkle with garlic salt. Place in the preheated air-fryer and air-fry for 4 minutes, turning halfway through cooking. Serve immediately.

Easy Cheesy Scrambled Eggs

Servings: 1
Cooking Time:xx
Ingredients:

- 1 tbsp butter
- 2 eggs
- 100g grated cheese
- 2 tbsp milk
- Salt and pepper for seasoning

Directions:

1. Add the butter inside the air fryer pan and cook at 220ºC until the butter has melted
2. Add the eggs and milk to a bowl and combine, seasoning to your liking
3. Pour the eggs into the butter panned cook for 3 minutes, stirring around lightly to scramble
4. Add the cheese and cook for another 2 more minutes

Tangy Breakfast Hash

Servings: 6
Cooking Time:xx
Ingredients:

- 2 tbsp olive oil
- 2 sweet potatoes, cut into cubes
- 1 tbsp smoked paprika
- 1 tsp salt
- 1 tsp black pepper
- 2 slices of bacon, cut into small pieces

Directions:

1. Preheat your air fryer to 200ºC
2. Pour the olive oil into a large mixing bowl

3. Add the bacon, seasonings, potatoes and toss to evenly coat
4. Transfer the mixture into the air fryer and cook for 12-16 minutes
5. Stir after 10 minutes and continue to stir periodically for another 5 minutes

Blueberry Bread

Servings: 8
Cooking Time:xx
Ingredients:

- 260ml milk
- 3 eggs
- 25g protein powder
- 400g frozen blueberries
- 600g bisquick or pancake mixture

Directions:

1. Take a large mixing bowl and combine all ingredients until smooth
2. Preheat the air fryer to 250ºC
3. Place the mixture into a loaf tin
4. Place the tin into the air fryer and cook for 30 minutes
5. A toothpick should come out clean if the bread is cooked

Your Favourite Breakfast Bacon

Servings: 2
Cooking Time:xx
Ingredients:

- 4-5 rashers of lean bacon, fat cut off
- Salt and pepper for seasoning

Directions:

1. Line your air fryer basket with parchment paper
2. Place the bacon in the basket
3. Set the fryer to 200ºC
4. Cook for 10 minutes for crispy. If you want it very crispy, cook for another 2 minutes

Easy Omelette

Servings: 1
Cooking Time:xx
Ingredients:

- 50ml milk
- 2 eggs
- 60g grated cheese, any you like
- Any garnishes you like, such as mushrooms, peppers, etc.

Directions:

1. Take a small mixing bowl and crack the eggs inside, whisking with the milk
2. Add the salt and garnishes and combine again
3. Grease a 6x3" pan and pour the mixture inside
4. Arrange the pan inside the air fryer basket
5. Cook at 170°C for 10 minutes
6. At the halfway point, sprinkle the cheese on top
7. Loosen the edges with a spatula before serving

Loaded Hash Browns

Servings: 4
Cooking Time:xx
Ingredients:

- 4 large potatoes
- 2 tbsp bicarbonate of soda
- 1 tbsp salt
- 1 tbsp black pepper
- 1 tsp cayenne pepper
- 2 tbsp olive oil
- 1 large chopped onion
- 1 chopped red pepper
- 1 chopped green pepper

Directions:

1. Grate the potatoes
2. Squeeze out any water contained within the potatoes
3. Take a large bowl of water and add the potatoes
4. Add the bicarbonate of soda, combine everything and leave to soak for 25 minutes
5. Drain the water away and carefully pat the potatoes to dry
6. Transfer your potatoes into another bowl
7. Add the spices and oil
8. Combining everything well, tossing to coat evenly
9. Place your potatoes into your fryer basket
10. Set to 200°C and cook for 10 minutes
11. Give the potatoes a shake and add the peppers and the onions
12. Cook for another 10 minutes

Avocado Fries

Servings: 2
Cooking Time:xx
Ingredients:

- 35 g/¼ cup plain/all-purpose flour (gluten free if you wish)
- ½ teaspoon chilli/chili powder
- 1 egg, beaten
- 50 g/heaped ½ cup dried breadcrumbs (gluten-free if you wish; see page 9)
- 1 avocado, skin and stone removed, and each half sliced lengthways
- salt and freshly ground black pepper

Directions:

1. Preheat the air-fryer to 200°C/400°F.
2. In a bowl combine the flour and chilli/chili powder, then season with salt and pepper. Place the beaten egg in a second bowl and the breadcrumbs in a third bowl.
3. Dip each avocado slice in the seasoned flour (shaking off any excess), then the egg and finally the breadcrumbs.
4. Add the breaded avocado slices to the preheated air-fryer and air-fry for 6 minutes, turning after 4 minutes. Serve immediately.

Swede Fries

Servings: 4
Cooking Time:xx
Ingredients:

- 1 medium swede/rutabaga
- ½ teaspoon salt
- ½ teaspoon freshly ground black pepper
- 1½ teaspoons dried thyme
- 1 tablespoon olive oil

Directions:

1. Preheat the air-fryer to 160°C/325°F.
2. Peel the swede/rutabaga and slice into fries about 6 x 1 cm/2½ x ½ in., then toss the fries in the salt, pepper, thyme and oil, making sure every fry is coated.
3. Tip into the preheated air-fryer in a single layer (you may need to cook them in two batches, depending on the size of your air-fryer) and air-fry for 15 minutes, shaking the drawer halfway through. Then increase the temperature to 180°C/350°F and cook for a further 5 minutes. Serve immediately.

Patatas Bravas

Servings: 4
Cooking Time:xx
Ingredients:

- 300g potatoes
- 1 tsp garlic powder
- 1 tbsp avocado oil
- 1 tbsp smoked paprika
- Salt and pepper to taste

Directions:

1. Peel the potatoes and cut them into cubes
2. Bring a large saucepan of water to the boil and add the potatoes, cooking for 6 minutes
3. Strain the potatoes and place them on a piece of kitchen towel, allowing to dry
4. Take a large mixing bowl and add the garlic powder, salt, and pepper and add the avocado oil, mixing together well
5. Add the potatoes to the bowl and coat liberally
6. Place the potatoes into the basket and arrange them with space in-between
7. Set your fryer to 200°C
8. Cook the potatoes for 15 minutes, giving them a shake at the halfway point
9. Remove and serve

Whole Mini Peppers

Servings: 2
Cooking Time:xx
Ingredients:

- 9 whole mini (bell) peppers
- 1 teaspoon olive oil
- ¼ teaspoon salt

Directions:

1. Preheat the air-fryer to 180°C/350°F.
2. Place the peppers in a baking dish that fits in for your air-fryer and drizzle over the oil, then sprinkle over the salt.
3. Add the dish to the preheated air-fryer and air-fry for 10–12 minutes, depending on how 'chargrilled' you like your peppers.

Potato Fries

Servings: 2
Cooking Time:xx
Ingredients:

- 2 large potatoes (baking potato size)
- 1 teaspoon olive oil
- salt

Directions:

1. Peel the potatoes and slice into fries about 5 x 1.5cm/¾ x ¾ in. by the length of the potato. Submerge the fries in a bowl of cold water and place in the fridge for about 10 minutes.
2. Meanwhile, preheat the air-fryer to 160°C/325°F.
3. Drain the fries thoroughly, then toss in the oil and season. Tip into the preheated air-fryer in a single layer (you may need to cook them in two batches, depending on the size of your air-fryer). Air-fry for 15 minutes, tossing once during cooking by shaking the air-fryer drawer, then increase the temperature of the air-fryer to 200°C/400°F and cook for a further 3 minutes. Serve immediately.

Delicious Breakfast Casserole

Servings: 4
Cooking Time:xx
Ingredients:

- 4 frozen hash browns
- 8 sausages, cut into pieces
- 4 eggs
- 1 diced yellow pepper
- 1 diced green pepper
- 1 diced red pepper
- Half a diced onion

Directions:

1. Line the bottom of your fryer with aluminium foil and arrange the hash browns inside
2. Add the sausage on top (uncooked)
3. Now add the onions and the peppers, sprinkling evenly
4. Cook the casserole on 170°C for around 10 minutes
5. Open your fryer and give the mixture a good stir
6. Combine the eggs in a small bowl and pour over the casserole, closing the lid
7. Cook for another 10 minutes on the same temperature
8. Serve with a little seasoning to taste

Healthy Breakfast Bagels

Servings: 2
Cooking Time:xx
Ingredients:

- 170g self raising flour
- 120ml plain yogurt
- 1 egg

Directions:

1. Take a large mixing bowl, combine the flour and the yogurt to create a dough
2. Cover a flat surface with a little extra flour and set the dough down
3. Create four separate and even balls
4. Roll each ball out into a rope shape and form a bagel with each
5. Take a small mixing bowl and whisk the egg
6. Brush the egg over the top of the bagel
7. Arrange the bagels inside your fryer evenly
8. Cook at 170°C for 10 minutes
9. Allow to cool before serving

Courgette Fries

Servings: 2
Cooking Time:xx
Ingredients:

- 1 courgette/zucchini
- 3 tablespoons plain/all-purpose flour (gluten-free if you wish)
- ¼ teaspoon salt
- ¼ teaspoon freshly ground black pepper
- 60 g/¾ cup dried breadcrumbs (gluten-free if you wish; see page 9)
- 1 teaspoon dried oregano
- 20 g/¼ cup finely grated Parmesan
- 1 egg, beaten

Directions:

1. Preheat the air-fryer to 180°C/350°F.
2. Slice the courgette/zucchini into fries about 1.5 x 1.5 x 5 cm/⅝ x ⅝ x 2 in.
3. Season the flour with salt and pepper. Combine the breadcrumbs with the oregano and Parmesan.
4. Dip the courgettes/zucchini in the flour (shaking off any excess flour), then the egg, then the seasoned breadcrumbs.
5. Add the fries to the preheated air-fryer and air-fry for 15 minutes. They should be crispy on the outside but soft on the inside. Serve immediately.

Blanket Breakfast Eggs

Servings: 2
Cooking Time:xx
Ingredients:

- 2 eggs
- 2 slices of sandwich bread
- Olive oil spray
- Salt and pepper to taste

Directions:

1. Preheat your air fryer to 190°C and spray with a little oil
2. Meanwhile, take your bread and cut a hole into the middle of each piece
3. Place one slice inside your fryer and crack one egg into the middle
4. Season with a little salt and pepper
5. Cook for 5 minutes, before turning over and cooking for a further 2 minutes
6. Remove the first slice and repeat the process with the remaining slice of bread and egg

Breakfast Doughnuts

Servings: 4
Cooking Time:xx
Ingredients:

- 1 packet of Pillsbury Grands
- 5 tbsp raspberry jam
- 1 tbsp melted butter
- 5 tbsp sugar

Directions:

1. Preheat your air fryer to 250°C
2. Place the Pillsbury Grands into the air fryer and cook for around 5m minutes
3. Remove and place to one side
4. Take a large bowl and add the sugar
5. Coat the doughnuts in the melted butter, coating evenly
6. Dip into the sugar and coat evenly once more
7. Using an icing bag, add the jam into the bag and pipe an even amount into each doughnut
8. Eat warm or cold

French Toast

Servings: 2
Cooking Time:xx
Ingredients:

- 2 beaten eggs
- 2 tbsp softened butter
- 4 slices of sandwich bread
- 1 tsp cinnamon
- 1 tsp nutmeg
- 1 tsp ground cloves
- 1 tsp maple syrup

Directions:

1. Preheat your fryer to 180°C
2. Take a bowl and add the eggs, salt, cinnamon, nutmeg, and cloves, combining well
3. Take your bread and butter each side, cutting into strips
4. Dip the bread slices into the egg mixture
5. Arrange each slice into the basket of your fryer
6. Cook for 2 minutes
7. Take the basket out and spray with a little cooking spray
8. Turn over the slices and place back into the fryer
9. Cook for 4 minutes
10. Remove and serve with maple syrup

Cheese Scones

Servings:12
Cooking Time:xx
Ingredients:

- ½ teaspoon baking powder
- 210 g/1½ cups self-raising/self-rising flour (gluten-free if you wish), plus extra for dusting
- 50 g/3½ tablespoons cold butter, cubed
- 125 g/1½ cups grated mature Cheddar
- a pinch of cayenne pepper
- a pinch of salt
- 100 ml/7 tablespoons milk, plus extra for brushing the tops of the scones

Directions:

1. Mix the baking powder with the flour in a bowl, then add the butter and rub into the flour to form a crumblike texture. Add the cheese, cayenne pepper and salt and stir. Then add the milk, a little at a time, and bring together into a ball of dough.
2. Dust your work surface with flour. Roll the dough flat until about 1.5 cm/⅝ in. thick. Cut

out the scones using a 6-cm/2½-in. diameter cookie cutter. Gather the offcuts into a ball, re-roll and cut more scones – you should get about 12 scones from the mixture. Place the scones on an air-fryer liner or a piece of pierced parchment paper.

3. Preheat the air-fryer to 180°C/350°F.
4. Add the scones to the preheated air-fryer and air-fry for 8 minutes, turning them over halfway to cook the other side. Remove and allow to cool a little, then serve warm.

Egg & Bacon Breakfast Cups

Servings: 8
Cooking Time:xx
Ingredients:

- 6 eggs
- 1 chopped red pepper
- 1 chopped green pepper
- 1 chopped yellow pepper
- 2 tbsp double cream
- 50g chopped spinach
- 50g grated cheddar cheese
- 50g grated mozzarella cheese
- 3 slices of cooked bacon, crumbled into pieces

Directions:

1. Take a large mixing bowl and crack the eggs
2. Add the cream and season with a little salt and pepper, combining everything well
3. Add the peppers, spinach, onions, both cheeses, and the crumbled bacon, combining everything once more
4. You will need silicone moulds or cups for this part, and you should pour equal amounts of the mixture into 8 cups
5. Cook at 150°C for around 12 or 15 minutes, until the eggs are cooked properly

Blueberry & Lemon Breakfast Muffins

Servings: 12
Cooking Time:xx
Ingredients:

- 315g self raising flour
- 65g sugar
- 120ml double cream
- 2 tbsp of light cooking oil
- 2 eggs
- 125g blueberries
- The zest and juice of a lemon
- 1 tsp vanilla

Directions:

1. Take a small bowl and mix the self raising flour and sugar together
2. Take another bowl and mix together the oil, juice, eggs, cream, and vanilla
3. Add this mixture to the flour mixture and blend together
4. Add the blueberries and fold
5. You will need individual muffin holders, silicone works best. Spoon the mixture into the holders
6. Cook at 150ºC for 10 minutes
7. Check at the halfway point to check they're not cooking too fast
8. Remove and allow to cool

Mexican Breakfast Burritos

Servings: 6
Cooking Time:xx
Ingredients:

- 6 scrambled eggs
- 6 medium tortillas
- Half a minced red pepper
- 8 sausages, cut into cubes and browned
- 4 pieces of bacon, pre-cooked and cut into pieces
- 65g grated cheese of your choice
- A small amount of olive oil for cooking

Directions:

1. Into a regular mixing bowl, combine the eggs, bell pepper, bacon pieces, the cheese, and the browned sausage, giving everything a good stir
2. Take your first tortilla and place half a cup of the mixture into the middle, folding up the top and bottom and rolling closed

3. Repeat until all your tortillas have been used
4. Arrange the burritos into the bottom of your fryer and spray with a little oil
5. Cook the burritos at 170ºC for 5 minutes

Raspberry Breakfast Pockets

Servings: 1
Cooking Time:xx
Ingredients:

- 2 slices of sandwich bread
- 1 tbsp soft cream cheese
- 1 tbsp raspberry jam
- 1 tbsp milk
- 1 egg

Directions:

1. Take one slice of the bread and add one tablespoon of jam into the middle
2. Take the second slice and add the cream cheese into the middle
3. Using a blunt knife, spread the jam and the cheese across the bread, but don't go to the outer edges
4. Take a small bowl and whisk the eggs and the milk together
5. Set your fryer to 190ºC and spray with a little oil
6. Dip your sandwich into the egg and arrange inside your fryer
7. Cook for 5 minutes on the first side, turn and cook for another 2 minutes

Pitta Pizza

Servings: 2
Cooking Time:xx
Ingredients:

- 2 round wholemeal pitta breads
- 3 tablespoons passata/strained tomatoes
- 4 tablespoons grated mozzarella
- 1 teaspoon dried oregano
- 1 teaspoon olive oil
- basil leaves, to serve

Directions:

1. Preheat the air-fryer to 200ºC/400ºF.
2. Pop the pittas into the preheated air-fryer and air-fry for 1 minute.
3. Remove the pittas from the air-fryer and spread a layer of the passata/strained tomatoes on the pittas, then scatter over the mozzarella, oregano and oil. Return to the air-fryer and air-

fry for a further 4 minutes. Scatter over the basil leaves and serve immediately.

Cheesy Sausage Breakfast Pockets

Servings: 2
Cooking Time:xx
Ingredients:

- 1 packet of regular puff pastry
- 4 sausages, cooked and crumbled into pieces
- 5 eggs
- 50g cooked bacon
- 50g grated cheddar cheese

Directions:

1. Scramble your eggs in your usual way
2. Add the sausage and the bacon as you are cooking the eggs and combine well
3. Take your pastry sheets and cut rectangular shapes
4. Add a little of the egg and meat mixture to one half of each pastry piece
5. Fold the rectangles over and use a fork to seal down the edges
6. Place your pockets into your air fryer and cook at 190°C for 10 minutes
7. Allow to cool before serving

Breakfast Eggs & Spinach

Servings: 4
Cooking Time:xx
Ingredients:

- 500g wilted, fresh spinach
- 200g sliced deli ham
- 1 tbsp olive oil
- 4 eggs
- 4 tsp milk
- Salt and pepper to taste
- 1 tbsp butter for cooking

Directions:

1. Preheat your air fryer to 180°C
2. You will need 4 small ramekin dishes, coated with a little butter
3. Arrange the wilted spinach, ham, 1 teaspoon of milk and 1 egg into each ramekin and season with a little salt and pepper
4. Place in the fryer 15 to 20 minutes, until the egg is cooked to your liking
5. Allow to cool before serving

Plantain Fries

Servings: 2
Cooking Time:xx
Ingredients:

- 1 ripe plantain (yellow and brown outside skin)
- 1 teaspoon olive oil
- ¼ teaspoon salt

Directions:

1. Preheat the air-fryer to 180°C/350°F.
2. Peel the plantain and slice into fries about 6 x 1 cm/2½ x ½ in. Toss the fries in oil and salt, making sure every fry is coated.
3. Tip into the preheated air-fryer in a single layer (you may need to cook them in two batches, depending on the size of your air-fryer) and air-fry for 13–14 minutes until brown on the outside and soft on the inside. Serve immediately.

Hard Boiled Eggs Air Fryer Style

Servings: 2
Cooking Time:xx
Ingredients:

- 4 large eggs
- 1 tsp cayenne pepper
- Salt and pepper for seasoning

Directions:

1. Preheat the air fryer to 220°C
2. Take a wire rack and place inside the air fryer
3. Lay the eggs on the rack
4. Cook for between 15-17 minutes, depending upon how you like your eggs
5. Remove from the fryer and place in a bowl of cold water for around 5 minutes
6. Peel and season with the cayenne and the salt and pepper

Healthy Stuffed Peppers

Servings: 2
Cooking Time:xx
Ingredients:

- 1 large bell pepper, deseeded and cut into halves
- 1 tsp olive oil
- 4 large eggs
- Salt and pepper to taste

Directions:

1. Take your peppers and rub a little olive oil on the edges
2. Into each pepper, crack one egg and season with salt and pepper
3. You will need to insert a trivet into your air fryer to hold the peppers, and then arrange the peppers evenly
4. Set your fryer to 200ºC and cook for 13 minutes
5. Once cooked, remove and serve with a little more seasoning, if required

Easy Cheese & Bacon Toasties

Servings: 2
Cooking Time:xx
Ingredients:

- 4 slices of sandwich bread
- 2 slices of cheddar cheese
- 5 slices of pre-cooked bacon
- 1 tbsp melted butter
- 2 slices of mozzarella cheese

Directions:

1. Take the bread and spread the butter onto one side of each slice
2. Place one slice of bread into the fryer basket, buttered side facing downwards
3. Place the cheddar on top, followed by the bacon, mozzarella and the other slice of bread on top, buttered side upwards
4. Set your fryer to 170ºC
5. Cook for 4 minutes and then turn over and cook for another 3 minutes
6. Serve whilst still hot

Polenta Fries

Servings: 6
Cooking Time:xx
Ingredients:

- 800 ml/scant 3½ cups water
- 1½ vegetable stock cubes
- ¾ teaspoon dried oregano
- ¾ teaspoon freshly ground black pepper
- 200 g/1⅓ cups quick-cook polenta/cornmeal
- 2 teaspoons olive oil
- 55 g/6 tablespoons plain/all-purpose flour (gluten-free if you wish)
- garlic mayonnaise, to serve

Directions:

1. Bring the water and stock cubes to the boil in a saucepan with the oregano and black pepper. Stir in the polenta/cornmeal and continue to stir until the mixture becomes significantly more solid and is hard to stir – this should take about 5–6 minutes.
2. Grease a 15 x 15-cm/6 x 6-in. baking pan with some of the olive oil. Tip the polenta into the baking pan, smoothing down with the back of a wet spoon. Leave to cool at room temperature for about 30 minutes, then pop into the fridge for at least an hour.
3. Remove the polenta from the fridge and carefully tip out onto a chopping board. Slice the polenta into fingers 7.5 x 1 x 2 cm/3 x ½ x ¾ in. Roll the polenta fingers in the flour, then spray or drizzle the remaining olive oil over the fingers.
4. Preheat the air-fryer to 200ºC/400ºF.
5. Lay the fingers apart from one another in a single layer in the preheated air-fryer (you may need to cook these in batches, depending on the size of your air-fryer). Air-fry for 9 minutes, turning once halfway through cooking. Serve immediately with garlic mayonnaise.

Muhammara

Servings: 4
Cooking Time:xx
Ingredients:

- 4 romano peppers
- 4 tablespoons olive oil
- 100 g/1 cup walnuts
- 90 g/1 heaped cup dried breadcrumbs (see page 9)
- 1 teaspoon cumin
- 2 tablespoons pomegranate molasses
- freshly squeezed juice of ½ a lemon
- ½ teaspoon chilli/chili salt (or salt and some chilli/hot red pepper flakes combined)

- fresh pomegranate seeds, to serve

Directions:
1. Preheat the air-fryer to 180ºC/350ºF.
2. Rub the peppers with ½ teaspoon of the olive oil. Add the peppers to the preheated air-fryer and air-fry for 8 minutes.
3. Meanwhile, lightly toast the walnuts by tossing them in a shallow pan over a medium heat for 3–5 minutes. Allow to cool, then grind the walnuts in a food processor. Once the peppers are cooked, chop off the tops and discard most of the seeds. Add to the food processor with all other ingredients. Process until smooth. Allow to cool in the fridge, then serve the dip with pomegranate seeds on top.

Crunchy Mexican Breakfast Wrap

Servings: 2
Cooking Time:xx
Ingredients:
- 2 large tortillas
- 2 corn tortillas
- 1 sliced jalapeño pepper
- 4 tbsp ranchero sauce
- 1 sliced avocado
- 25g cooked pinto beans

Directions:
1. Take each of your large tortillas and add the egg, jalapeño, sauce, the corn tortillas, the avocado and the pinto beans, in that order. If you want to add more sauce at this point, you can
2. Fold over your wrap to make sure that nothing escapes
3. Place each wrap into your fryer and cook at 190ºC for 6 minutes
4. Remove your wraps and place in the oven, cooking for a further 5 minutes at 180ºC, until crispy
5. Place each wrap into a frying pan and crisp a little more on a low heat, for a couple of minutes on each side

Baba Ganoush

Servings: 4
Cooking Time:xx
Ingredients:
- 1 large aubergine/eggplant, sliced in half lengthways

- ½ teaspoon salt
- 5 tablespoons olive oil
- 1 bulb garlic
- 30 g/2 tablespoons tahini or nut butter
- 2 tablespoons freshly squeezed lemon juice
- ½ teaspoon ground cumin
- ¼ teaspoon smoked paprika
- salt and freshly ground black pepper
- 3 tablespoons freshly chopped flat-leaf parsley

Directions:
1. Preheat the air-fryer to 200ºC/400ºF.
2. Lay the aubergine/eggplant halves cut side up. Sprinkle over the salt, then drizzle over 1 tablespoon of oil. Cut the top off the garlic bulb, brush the exposed cloves with a little olive oil, then wrap in foil. Place the aubergine/eggplant and foil-wrapped garlic in the preheated air-fryer and air-fry for 15–20 minutes until the inside of the aubergine is soft and buttery in texture.
3. Scoop the flesh of the aubergine into a bowl. Squeeze out about 1 tablespoon of the cooked garlic and add to the bowl with the remaining 4 tablespoons of olive oil, the tahini/nut butter, lemon juice, spices and salt and pepper to taste. Mix well and serve with fresh flat-leaf parsley sprinkled over.

Morning Sausage Wraps

Servings: 8
Cooking Time:xx
Ingredients:
- 8 sausages, chopped into pieces
- 2 slices of cheddar cheese, cut into quarters
- 1 can of regular crescent roll dough
- 8 wooden skewers

Directions:
1. Take the dough and separate each one
2. Cut open the sausages evenly
3. The one of your crescent rolls and on the widest part, add a little sausage and then a little cheese
4. Roll the dough and tuck it until you form a triangle
5. Repeat this for four times and add into your air fryer
6. Cook at 190ºC for 3 minutes
7. Remove your dough and add a skewer for serving
8. Repeat with the other four pieces of dough

Breakfast "pop Tarts"

Servings: 6
Cooking Time:xx
Ingredients:

- 2 slices of prepared pie crust, shortbread or filo will work fine
- 2 tbsp strawberry jam
- 60ml plain yogurt
- 1 tsp cornstarch
- 1 tsp Stevia sweetener
- 2 tbsp cream cheese
- A drizzle of olive oil

Directions:

1. Lay your pie crust flat and cut into 6 separate rectangular pieces
2. In a small bowl, mix together the cornstarch and the jam
3. Spread 1 tablespoon of the mixture on top of the crust
4. Fold each crust over to form the tart
5. Seal down the edges using a fork
6. Arrange your tarts inside the frying basket and spray with a little olive oil
7. Heat to 175°C and cook for 10 minutes
8. Meanwhile, combine the yogurt, cream cheese and Stevia in a bowl
9. Remove the tarts and allow to cool
10. Once cool, add the frosting on top and sprinkle with the sugar sprinkles

Cumin Shoestring Carrots

Servings: 2
Cooking Time:xx
Ingredients:

- 300 g/10½ oz. carrots
- 1 teaspoon cornflour/cornstarch
- 1 teaspoon ground cumin
- ¼ teaspoon salt
- 1 tablespoon olive oil
- garlic mayonnaise, to serve

Directions:

1. Preheat the air-fryer to 200°C/400°F.
2. Peel the carrots and cut into thin fries, roughly 10 cm x 1 cm x 5 mm/4 x ½ x ¼ in. Toss the carrots in a bowl with all the other ingredients.
3. Add the carrots to the preheated air-fryer and air-fry for 9 minutes, shaking the drawer of the air-fryer a couple of times during cooking. Serve with garlic mayo on the side.

Breakfast Sausage Burgers

Servings: 2
Cooking Time:xx
Ingredients:

- 8 links of your favourite sausage
- Salt and pepper to taste

Directions:

1. Remove the sausage from the skins and use a fork to create a smooth mixture
2. Season to your liking
3. Shape the sausage mixture into burgers or patties
4. Preheat your air fryer to 260°C
5. Arrange the burgers in the fryer, so they are not touching each other
6. Cook for 8 minutes
7. Serve still warm

Meaty Egg Cups

Servings: 4
Cooking Time:xx
Ingredients:

- 8 slices of toasted sandwich bread
- 2 slices of ham
- 4 eggs
- Salt and pepper to taste
- Butter for greasing

Directions:

1. Take 4 ramekins and grease the insides with a little butter
2. Flatten the slices of toast with a rolling pin and arrange inside the ramekins - two in each
3. Line the inside of each ramekin with a slice of ham
4. Crack one egg into each ramekin
5. Season with a little salt and pepper
6. Place the ramekins into the air fryer and cook at 160°C for 15 minutes
7. Remove from the fryer and wait to cool just slightly
8. Remove and serve

Halloumi Fries

Servings: 2
Cooking Time:xx
Ingredients:

- 225 g/8 oz. halloumi
- 40 g/heaped ¼ cup plain/all-purpose flour (gluten-free if you wish)
- ½ teaspoon sweet smoked paprika
- ½ teaspoon dried oregano
- ¼ teaspoon mild chilli/chili powder
- olive oil or avocado oil, for spraying

Directions:

1. Preheat the air-fryer to 180ºC/350ºF.
2. Slice the halloumi into fries roughly 2 x 1.5 cm/¾ x ⅝ in.
3. Mix the flour and seasoning in a bowl and dip each halloumi stick into the flour to coat. Spray with a little oil.
4. Add the fries to the preheated air-fryer and air-fry for 5 minutes. Serve immediately.

Sweet Potato Fries

Servings: 4
Cooking Time:xx
Ingredients:

- 2 medium sweet potatoes
- 2 teaspoons olive oil
- ½ teaspoon salt
- ½ teaspoon chilli/hot red pepper flakes
- ½ teaspoon smoked paprika

Directions:

1. Preheat the air-fryer to 190ºC/375ºF.
2. Peel the sweet potatoes and slice into fries about 1 x 1 cm/½ x ½ in. by the length of the potato. Toss the sweet potato fries in the oil, salt, chilli and paprika, making sure every fry is coated.
3. Tip into the preheated air-fryer in a single layer (you may need to cook them in two batches, depending on the size of your air-fryer). Air-fry for 10 minutes, turning once halfway during cooking. Serve immediately.

Monte Cristo Breakfast Sandwich

Servings: 4
Cooking Time:xx
Ingredients:

- 1 egg
- 2 slices of sandwich bread
- 1/4 tsp vanilla extract
- 4 slices of sliced Swiss cheese
- 4 slices of sliced deli ham
- 4 slices of sliced turkey
- 1 tsp melted butter
- Powdered sugar for serving

Directions:

1. In a small bowl, mix together the egg and vanilla extract, combining well
2. Take your bread and assemble your sandwich, starting with a slice of cheese, then the ham, turkey, and then another slice of the cheese, with the other slice of bread on the top
3. Compress the sandwich a little, so it cooks better
4. Take a piece of cooking foil and brush over it with the butter
5. Take your sandwich and dip each side into the egg mixture, leaving it to one side for around half a minute
6. Place the sandwich on the foil and place it inside your fryer
7. Cook at 200ºC for around 10 minutes, before turning the sandwich over and cooking for another 8 minutes
8. Transfer your sandwich onto a plate and sprinkle with a little powdered sugar

Apple Crisps

Servings: 2
Cooking Time:xx
Ingredients:

- 2 apples, chopped
- 1 tsp cinnamon
- 2 tbsp brown sugar
- 1 tsp lemon juice
- 2.5 tbsp plain flour
- 3 tbsp oats
- 2 tbsp cold butter
- Pinch of salt

Directions:

1. Preheat the air fryer to 260ºC
2. Take a 5" baking dish and crease
3. Take a large bowl and combine the apples with the sugar, cinnamon and lemon juice
4. Add the mixture to the baking dish and cover with aluminium foil
5. Place in the air fryer and cook for 15 minutes

6. Open the lid and cook for another 5 minutes
7. Combine the rest of the ingredients in a food processor, until a crumble-type mixture occurs
8. Add over the top of the cooked apples
9. Cook with the lid open for another 5 minutes
10. Allow to cool a little before serving

Easy Air Fryer Sausage

Servings: 5
Cooking Time:xx
Ingredients:
- 5 uncooked sausages
- 1 tbsp mustard
- Salt and pepper for seasoning

Directions:
1. Line the basket of your fryer with parchment paper
2. Arrange the sausages inside the basket
3. Set to 180°C and cook for 15 minutes
4. Turn the sausages over and cook for another 5 minutes
5. Remove and cool
6. Drizzle the mustard over the top and season to your liking

Toad In The Hole, Breakfast Style

Servings: 4

Cooking Time:xx
Ingredients:
- 1 sheet of puff pastry (defrosted)
- 4 eggs
- 4 tbsp grated cheese (cheddar works well)
- 4 slices of cooked ham, cut into pieces
- Chopped fresh herbs of your choice

Directions:
1. Preheat your air fryer to 200°C
2. Take your pastry sheet and place it on a flat surface, cutting it into four pieces
3. Take two of the pastry sheets and place them inside your fryer, cooking for up to 8 minutes, until done
4. Remove the pastry and flatten the centre down with a spoon, to form a deep hole
5. Add a tablespoon of the cheese and a tablespoon of the ham into the hole
6. Crack one egg into the hole
7. Return the pastry to the air fryer and cook for another 6 minutes, or until the egg is done as you like it
8. Remove and allow to cool
9. Repeat the process with the rest of the pastry remaining
10. Sprinkle fresh herbs on top and serve

Fish & Seafood Recipes

Coconut Shrimp

Servings: 4
Cooking Time:xx
Ingredients:
- 250g flour
- 1 ½ tsp black pepper
- 2 eggs
- 150g unsweetened flaked coconut
- 1 Serrano chilli, thinly sliced
- 25g panko bread crumbs

- 300g shrimp raw
- ½ tsp salt
- 4 tbsp honey
- 25ml lime juice

Directions:
1. Mix together flour and pepper, in another bowl beat the eggs and in another bowl mix the panko and coconut
2. Dip each of the shrimp in the flour mix then the egg and then cover in the coconut mix
3. Coat the shrimp in cooking spray
4. Place in the air fryer and cook at 200°C for 6-8 mins turning half way through

5. Mix together the honey, lime juice and chilli and serve with the shrimp

Thai Salmon Patties

Servings: 7
Cooking Time:xx
Ingredients:

- 1 large can of salmon, drained and bones removed
- 30g panko breadcrumbs
- ¼ tsp salt
- 1 ½ tbsp Thai red curry paste
- 1 ½ tbsp brown sugar
- Zest of 1 lime
- 2 eggs
- Cooking spray

Directions:

1. Take a large bowl and combine all ingredients together until smooth
2. Use your hands to create patties that are around 1 inch in thickness
3. Preheat your air fryer to 180°C
4. Coat the patties with cooking spray
5. Cook for 4 minutes each side

Garlic Butter Salmon

Servings: 2
Cooking Time:xx
Ingredients:

- 2 salmon fillets, boneless with the skin left on
- 1 tsp minced garlic
- 2 tbsp melted butter
- 1 tsp chopped parsley
- Salt and pepper to taste

Directions:

1. Preheat the air fryer to 270 °C
2. Take a bowl and combine the melted butter, parsley and garlic to create a sauce
3. Season the salmon to your liking
4. Brush the salmon with the garlic mixture, on both sides
5. Place the salmon into the fryer, with the skin side facing down
6. Cook for 10 minutes - the salmon is done when it flakes with ease

Fish Sticks With Tartar Sauce Batter

Servings: 4
Cooking Time:xx
Ingredients:

- 6 tbsp mayonnaise
- 2 tbsp dill pickle
- 1 tsp seafood seasoning
- 400g cod fillets, cut into sticks
- 300g panko breadcrumbs

Directions:

1. Combine the mayonnaise, seafood seasoning and dill pickle in a large bowl.
2. Add the cod sticks and coat well
3. Preheat air fryer to 200°C
4. Coat the fish sticks in the breadcrumbs
5. Place in the air fryer and cook for 12 minutes

Store-cupboard Fishcakes

Servings: 3
Cooking Time:xx
Ingredients:

- 400 g/14 oz. cooked potato – either mashed potato or the insides of jacket potatoes (see page 124)
- 2 x 150–200-g/5½–7-oz. cans fish, such as tuna or salmon, drained
- 2 eggs
- ¾ teaspoon salt
- 1 teaspoon dried parsley
- ½ teaspoon freshly ground black pepper
- 1 tablespoon olive oil
- caper dressing (see page 79), to serve

Directions:

1. Mix the cooked potato, fish, eggs, salt, parsley and pepper together in a bowl, then divide into 6 equal portions and form into fishcakes. Drizzle the olive oil over both sides of each fishcake.
2. Preheat the air-fryer to 180°C/350°F.
3. Add the fishcakes to the preheated air-fryer and air-fry for 15 minutes, turning halfway through cooking. Serve with salad and tartare sauce or Caper Dressing.

Oat & Parmesan Crusted Fish Fillets

Servings: 2
Cooking Time:xx
Ingredients:

- 20 g/⅓ cup fresh breadcrumbs
- 25 g/3 tablespoons oats
- 15 g/¼ cup grated Parmesan
- 1 egg
- 2 x 175-g/6-oz. white fish fillets, skin-on
- salt and freshly ground black pepper

Directions:

1. Preheat the air-fryer to 180°C/350°F.
2. Combine the breadcrumbs, oats and cheese in a bowl and stir in a pinch of salt and pepper. In another bowl beat the egg. Dip the fish fillets in the egg, then top with the oat mixture.
3. Add the fish fillets to the preheated air-fryer on an air-fryer liner or a piece of pierced parchment paper. Air-fry for 10 minutes. Check the fish is just flaking away when a fork is inserted, then serve immediately.

Copycat Fish Fingers

Servings: 2
Cooking Time:xx
Ingredients:

- 2 slices wholemeal bread, grated into breadcrumbs
- 50g plain flour
- 1 beaten egg
- 1 white fish fillet
- The juice of 1 small lemon
- 1 tsp parsley
- 1 tsp thyme
- 1 tsp mixed herbs
- Salt and pepper to taste

Directions:

1. Preheat the air fryer to 180°C
2. Add salt pepper and parsley to the breadcrumbs and combine well
3. Place the egg in another bowl
4. Place the flour in a separate bowl
5. Place the fish into a food processor and add the lemon juice, salt, pepper thyme and mixed herbs
6. Blitz to create a crumb-like consistency

7. Roll your fish in the flour, then the egg and then the breadcrumbs
8. Cook at 180°C for 8 minutes

Fish In Foil

Servings: 2
Cooking Time:xx
Ingredients:

- 1 tablespoon avocado oil or olive oil, plus extra for greasing
- 1 tablespoon soy sauce (or tamari)
- 1½ teaspoons freshly grated garlic
- 1½ teaspoons freshly grated ginger
- 1 small red chilli/chile, finely chopped
- 2 skinless, boneless white fish fillets (about 350 g/12 oz. total weight)

Directions:

1. Mix the oil, soy sauce, garlic, ginger and chilli/chile together. Brush a little oil onto two pieces of foil, then lay the fish in the centre of the foil. Spoon the topping mixture over the fish. Wrap the foil around the fish to make a parcel, with a gap above the fish but shallow enough to fit in your air-fryer basket.
2. Preheat the air-fryer to 180°C/350°F.
3. Add the foil parcels to the preheated air-fryer and air-fry for 7–10 minutes, depending on the thickness of your fillets. The fish should just flake when a fork is inserted. Serve immediately.

Ranch Style Fish Fillets

Servings: 4
Cooking Time:xx
Ingredients:

- 200g bread crumbs
- 30g ranch-style dressing mix
- 2 tbsp oil
- 2 beaten eggs
- 4 fish fillets of your choice
- Lemon wedges to garnish

Directions:

1. Preheat air fryer to 180°C
2. Mix the bread crumbs and ranch dressing mix together, add in the oil until the mix becomes crumbly
3. Dip the fish into the, then cover in the breadcrumb mix
4. Place in the air fryer and cook for 12-13 minutes

Lobster Tails

Servings: 2
Cooking Time:xx
Ingredients:

- 4 lobster tails
- 2 tbsp melted butter
- ½ tsp salt
- 1 tsp pepper

Directions:

1. Cut the lobster tails through the tail section and pull back the shell
2. Brush with the melted butter and sprinkle with salt and pepper
3. Heat the air fryer to 200°C and cook for 4 minutes
4. Brush with melted butter and cook for a further 2 minutes

Air Fryer Tuna

Servings: 2
Cooking Time:xx
Ingredients:

- 2 tuna steaks, boneless and skinless
- 2 tsp honey
- 1 tsp grated ginger
- 4 tbsp soy sauce
- 1 tsp sesame oil
- 1/2 tsp rice vinegar

Directions:

1. Combine the honey, soy sauce, rice vinegar and sesame oil in a bowl until totally mixed together
2. Cover the tuna steaks with the sauce and place in the refrigerator for half an hour to marinade
3. Preheat the air fryer to 270°C
4. Cook the tuna for 4 minutes
5. Allow to rest before slicing

Pesto Salmon

Servings: 4
Cooking Time:xx
Ingredients:

- 4 x 150–175-g/5½–6-oz. salmon fillets
- lemon wedges, to serve
- PESTO
- 50 g/scant ½ cup toasted pine nuts
- 50 g/2 oz. fresh basil
- 50 g/⅔ cup grated Parmesan or Pecorino
- 100 ml/7 tablespoons olive oil

Directions:

1. To make the pesto, blitz the pine nuts, basil and Parmesan to a paste in a food processor. Pour in the olive oil and process again.
2. Preheat the air-fryer to 160°C/325°F.
3. Top each salmon fillet with 2 tablespoons of the pesto. Add the salmon fillets to the preheated air-fryer and air-fry for 9 minutes. Check the internal temperature of the fish has reached at least 63°C/145°F using a meat thermometer – if not, cook for another few minutes.

Shrimp Wrapped With Bacon

Servings: 2
Cooking Time:xx
Ingredients:

- 16 shrimp
- 16 slices of bacon
- 2 tbsp ranch dressing to serve

Directions:

1. Preheat the air fryer to 200°C
2. Wrap the shrimps in the bacon
3. Refrigerate for 30 minutes
4. Cook the shrimp for about 5 minutes turn them over and cook for a further 2 minutes
5. Serve with the ranch dressing on the side

Salmon Patties

Servings: 4
Cooking Time:xx
Ingredients:

- 400g salmon
- 1 egg
- 1 diced onion
- 200g breadcrumbs
- 1 tsp dill weed

Directions:

1. Remove all bones and skin from the salmon
2. Mix egg, onion, dill weed and bread crumbs with the salmon
3. Shape mixture into patties and place into the air fryer
4. Set air fryer to 180°C
5. Cook for 5 minutes then turn them over and cook for a further 5 minutes until golden brown

Fish In Parchment Paper

Servings: 2
Cooking Time:xx
Ingredients:

- 250g cod fillets
- 1 chopped carrot
- 1 chopped fennel
- 1 tbsp oil
- 1 thinly sliced red pepper
- ½ tsp tarragon
- 1 tbsp lemon juice
- 1 tbsp salt
- ½ tsp ground pepper

Directions:

1. In a bowl, mix the tarragon and ½ tsp salt add the vegetables and mix well
2. Cut two large squares of parchment paper
3. Spray the cod with oil and cover both sides with salt and pepper
4. Place the cod in the parchment paper and add the vegetables
5. Fold over the paper to hold the fish and vegetables
6. Place in the air fryer and cook at 170°C for 15 minutes

Cod In Parma Ham

Servings: 2
Cooking Time:xx
Ingredients:

- 2 x 175–190-g/6–7-oz. cod fillets, skin removed
- 6 slices Parma ham or prosciutto
- 16 cherry tomatoes
- 60 g/2 oz. rocket/arugula
- DRESSING
- 1 tablespoon olive oil
- 1½ teaspoons balsamic vinegar
- garlic salt, to taste
- freshly ground black pepper, to taste

Directions:

1. Preheat the air-fryer to 180°C/350°F.
2. Wrap each piece of cod snugly in 3 ham slices. Add the ham-wrapped cod fillets and the tomatoes to the preheated air-fryer and air-fry for 6 minutes, turning the cod halfway through cooking. Check the internal temperature of the fish has reached at least 60°C/140°F using a meat thermometer – if not, cook for another minute.
3. Meanwhile, make the dressing by combining all the ingredients in a jar and shaking well.
4. Serve the cod and tomatoes on a bed of rocket/arugula with the dressing poured over.

Sea Bass With Asparagus Spears

Servings: 2
Cooking Time:xx
Ingredients:

- 2 x 100-g/3½-oz. sea bass fillets
- 8 asparagus spears
- 2 teaspoons olive oil
- salt and freshly ground black pepper
- boiled new potatoes, to serve
- CAPER DRESSING
- 1½ tablespoons olive oil
- grated zest and freshly squeezed juice of ½ lemon
- 1 tablespoon small, jarred capers
- 1 teaspoon Dijon mustard
- 1 tablespoon freshly chopped flat-leaf parsley

Directions:

1. Preheat the air-fryer to 180°C/350°F.
2. Prepare the fish and asparagus by brushing both with the olive oil and sprinkling over salt and pepper.
3. Add the asparagus to the preheated air-fryer and air-fry for 4 minutes, then turn the asparagus and add the fish to the air-fryer drawer. Cook for a further 4 minutes. Check the internal temperature of the fish has reached at least 60°C/140°F using a meat thermometer – if not, cook for another minute.
4. Meanwhile, make the dressing by combining all the ingredients in a jar and shaking well. Pour the dressing over the cooked fish and asparagus spears and serve with new potatoes.

Beer Battered Fish Tacos

Servings: 2
Cooking Time:xx
Ingredients:

- 300g cod fillets
- 2 eggs
- 1 can of Mexican beer
- 300g cornstarch
- 300g flour
- 2 soft corn tortillas
- ½ tsp chilli powder
- 1 tbsp cumin
- Salt and pepper to taste

Directions:

1. Whisk together the eggs and beer
2. In a separate bowl whisk together cornstarch, chilli powder, flour, cumin and salt and pepper
3. Coat the fish in the egg mixture then coat in flour mixture
4. Spray the air fryer with non stick spray and add the fish
5. Set your fryer to 170ºC and cook for 15 minutes
6. Place the fish in a corn tortilla

Chilli Lime Tilapia

Servings: 3
Cooking Time:xx
Ingredients:

- 500g Tilapia fillets
- 25g panko crumbs
- 200g flour
- Salt and pepper to taste
- 2 eggs
- 1 tbsp chilli powder
- The juice of 1 lime

Directions:

1. Mix panko, salt and pepper and chilli powder together
2. Whisk the egg in a separate bowl
3. Spray the air fryer with cooking spray
4. Dip the tilapia in the flour, then in the egg and cover in the panko mix
5. Place fish in the air fryer, spray with cooking spray and cook for 7-8 minutes at 190ºC
6. Turn the fish over and cook for a further 7-8 minutes until golden brown.
7. Squeeze lime juice over the top and serve

Shrimp With Yum Yum Sauce

Servings: 4
Cooking Time:xx
Ingredients:

- 400g peeled jumbo shrimp
- 1 tbsp soy sauce
- 1 tbsp garlic paste
- 1 tbsp ginger paste
- 4 tbsp mayo
- 2 tbsp ketchup
- 1 tbsp sugar
- 1 tsp paprika
- 1 tsp garlic powder

Directions:

1. Mix soy sauce, garlic paste and ginger paste in a bowl. Add the shrimp, allow to marinate for 15 minutes
2. In another bowl mix ketchup, mayo, sugar, paprika and the garlic powder to make the yum yum sauce.
3. Set the air fryer to 200ºC, place shrimp in the basket and cook for 8-10 minutes

Garlic-parsley Prawns

Servings: 2
Cooking Time:xx
Ingredients:

- 300 g/10½ oz. raw king prawns/jumbo shrimp (without shell)
- 40 g/3 tablespoons garlic butter, softened (see page 72)
- 2 tablespoons freshly chopped flat-leaf parsley

Directions:

1. Thread the prawns/shrimp onto 6 metal skewers that will fit your air-fryer. Mix together the softened garlic butter and parsley and brush evenly onto the prawn skewers.
2. Preheat the air-fryer to 180ºC/350ºF.
3. Place the skewers on an air-fryer liner or a piece of pierced parchment paper. Add the skewers to the preheated air-fryer and air-fry for 2 minutes, then turn the skewers over and cook for a further 2 minutes. Check the internal temperature of the prawns has reached at least 50ºC/120ºF using a meat thermometer – if not, cook for another few minutes and serve.

Honey Sriracha Salmon

Servings: 2
Cooking Time:xx
Ingredients:

- 25g sriracha
- 25g honey
- 500g salmon fillets
- 1 tbsp soy sauce

Directions:

1. Mix the honey, soy sauce and sriracha, keep half the mix to one side for dipping
2. Place the salmon in the sauce skin side up and marinade for 30 minutes
3. Spray air fryer basket with cooking spray
4. Heat the air fryer to 200ºC
5. Place salmon in the air fryer skin side down and cook for 12 minutes

Thai-style Tuna Fishcakes

Servings: 2
Cooking Time:xx
Ingredients:

- 200 g/7 oz. cooked potato
- 145 g/5 oz. canned tuna, drained
- 60 g/1 cup canned sweetcorn/corn kernels (drained weight)
- ½ teaspoon soy sauce
- ½ teaspoon fish sauce
- ½ teaspoon Thai 7 spice
- freshly squeezed juice of ½ a lime
- 1 teaspoon freshly grated garlic
- 1 teaspoon freshly grated ginger
- avocado or olive oil, for brushing
- LIME-ALMOND SATAY SAUCE
- 20 ml/4 teaspoons fresh lime juice
- 2 heaped tablespoons almond butter
- 1 teaspoon soy sauce
- ½ teaspoon freshly grated ginger
- ½ teaspoon freshly grated garlic
- ½ teaspoon avocado or olive oil
- ½ teaspoon maple syrup

Directions:

1. Combine all the fishcake ingredients in a food processor and blend together. Divide the mixture into 6 equal portions and mould into fishcakes. Brush a little oil over the top surface of the fishcakes.
2. Preheat the air-fryer to 180ºC/350ºF.
3. Place the fishcakes on an air-fryer liner or a piece of pierced parchment paper and add to the preheated air-fryer. Air-fry for 4 minutes, then turn over and brush the other side of each fishcake with oil and air-fry for a further 4 minutes.
4. To make the satay dipping sauce, mix all ingredients in a bowl with 1 tablespoon warm water. Serve alongside the fishcakes.

Cajun Prawn Skewers

Servings: 2
Cooking Time:xx
Ingredients:

- 350 g/12 oz. king prawns/jumbo shrimp
- MARINADE
- 1 teaspoon smoked paprika
- 1 teaspoon unrefined sugar
- 1 teaspoon salt
- ½ teaspoon onion powder
- ½ teaspoon mustard powder
- ¼ teaspoon dried oregano
- ¼ teaspoon dried thyme
- 1 teaspoon white wine vinegar
- 2 teaspoons olive oil

Directions:

1. Mix all the marinade ingredients together in a bowl. Mix the prawns/shrimp into the marinade and cover. Place in the fridge to marinate for at least an hour.
2. Preheat the air-fryer to 180ºC/350ºF.
3. Thread 4–5 prawns/shrimp on to each skewer (you should have enough for 4–5 skewers). Add the skewers to the preheated air-fryer and air-fry for 2 minutes, then turn the skewers and cook for a further 2 minutes. Check the internal temperature of the prawns/shrimp has reached at least 50ºC/125ºF using a meat thermometer – if not, cook for another few minutes. Serve immediately.

Salt & Pepper Calamari

Servings: 2
Cooking Time:xx
Ingredients:

- 500g squid rings
- 500g panko breadcrumbs
- 250g plain flour
- 2 tbsp pepper
- 2 tbsp salt
- 200ml buttermilk
- 1 egg

Directions:

1. Take a medium bowl and combine the buttermilk and egg, stirring well
2. Take another bowl and combine the salt, pepper, flour, and panko breadcrumbs, combining again
3. Dip the quid into the buttermilk first and then the breadcrumbs, coating evenly
4. Place in the air fryer basket
5. Cook at 150°C for 12 minutes, until golden

Lemon Pepper Shrimp

Servings: 2
Cooking Time:xx
Ingredients:

- ½ tbsp olive oil
- The juice of 1 lemon
- ¼ tsp paprika
- 1 tsp lemon pepper
- ¼ tsp garlic powder
- 400g uncooked shrimp
- 1 sliced lemon

Directions:

1. Preheat air fryer to 200°C
2. Mix olive oil, lemon juice, paprika, lemon pepper and garlic powder. Add the shrimp and mix well
3. Place shrimp in the air fryer and cook for 6-8 minutes until pink and firm.
4. Serve with lemon slices

Extra Crispy Popcorn Shrimp

Servings: 2
Cooking Time:xx
Ingredients:

- 300g Frozen popcorn shrimp
- 1 tsp cayenne pepper
- Salt and pepper for seasoning

Directions:

1. Preheat the air fryer to 220°C
2. Place the shrimp inside the air fryer and cook for 6 minutes, giving them a shake at the halfway point
3. Remove and season with salt and pepper, and the cayenne to your liking

Air Fryer Mussels

Servings: 2
Cooking Time:xx
Ingredients:

- 400g mussels
- 1 tbsp butter
- 200ml water
- 1 tsp basil
- 2 tsp minced garlic
- 1 tsp chives
- 1 tsp parsley

Directions:

1. Preheat air fryer to 200°C
2. Clean the mussels, soak for 30 minutes, and remove the beard
3. Add all ingredients to an air fryer-safe pan
4. Cook for 3 minutes
5. Check to see if the mussels have opened, if not cook for a further 2 minutes. Once all mussels are open, they are ready to eat.

Maine Seafood

Servings: 2
Cooking Time:xx
Ingredients:

- 500g flour
- 400g breadcrumbs
- 300g steamer clams
- 3 eggs
- 3 tbsp water

Directions:

1. Soak the clams for 3 hours, drain and rinse
2. Bring 1 inch of water to boil, add the clams and cover with a lid, steam for about 7 minutes until the clams open.
3. Remove the clams from the shell and set aside
4. Put the eggs in a bowl and mix with the water
5. Dip the clams in the flour, then the egg and then coat in breadcrumbs
6. Heat the air fryer to 180°C and cook for about 7 minutes

Cajun Shrimp Boil

Servings: 6
Cooking Time:xx
Ingredients:
- 300g cooked shrimp
- 14 slices of smoked sausage
- 5 par boiled potatoes, cut into halves
- 4 mini corn on the cobs, quartered
- 1 diced onion
- 3 tbsp old bay seasoning
- Olive oil spray

Directions:
1. Combine all the ingredients in a bowl and mix well
2. Line the air fryer with foil
3. Place half the mix into the air fryer and cook at 200ºC for about 6 minutes, mix the ingredients and cook for a further 6 minutes.
4. Repeat for the second batch

Furikake Salmon

Servings: 2
Cooking Time:xx
Ingredients:
- 1 salmon fillet
- 2 tbsp furikake
- 150ml mayonnaise
- 1 tbsp shoe
- Salt and pepper for seasoning

Directions:
1. Preheat the air fryer to 230ºC
2. Take a small bowl and combine the mayonnaise and shoyu
3. Add salt and pepper to the salmon on both sides
4. Place in the air fryer with the skin facing downwards
5. Brush a layer of the mayonnaise mixture on top of the salmon
6. Sprinkle the furikake on top
7. Cook for 10 minutes

Cod Nuggets

Servings: 4
Cooking Time:xx
Ingredients:
- 400g cod fillets, cut into 8 chunks
- 35g flour
- 1 tbsp vegetable oil
- 200g cornflakes or cracker crumbs
- Egg wash - 1 tbsp egg and 1 tbsp water
- Salt and pepper to taste

Directions:
1. Crush the crackers or cornflakes to make crumbs, mix in the vegetable oil
2. Season the cod with salt and pepper and cover in flour, dip into the egg-wash then cover in crumbs
3. Set the air fryer to 180ºC
4. Place the cod nuggets in the air fryer basket and cook for 15 minutes, until golden brown.

Tandoori Salmon

Servings: 4
Cooking Time:xx
Ingredients:
- 300g salmon
- 1 tbsp butter
- 1 tbsp tandoori spice
- Salt and pepper to taste
- 1 small tomato
- Half a red onion
- 600g plain yogurt
- 30 fresh mint leaves, chopped
- 1 tsp minced green chilli
- 1 tbsp ground cumin
- Half a cucumber, chopped

Directions:
1. Cut the salmon into cubes and coat in the tandoori spice mix. Chill for 30 minutes to marinate
2. Blend mint, cumin and chilli with ¼ of the yogurt refrigerate and leave to steep
3. Peel the tomato and cut into cubes. Peel the cucumber and chop into cubes, finely dice the onion
4. Cook the salmon in the air fryer for 5-6 minutes at 200ºC
5. Mix the flavoured yogurt with the remaining yogurt, tomato, cucumber and onion
6. Place the sauce in serving bowls and place the salmon on top

Baked Panko Cod

Servings: 5
Cooking Time:xx

Ingredients:

- 400g cod, cut into 5 pieces
- 250g panko breadcrumbs
- 1 egg plus 1 egg white extra
- Cooking spray
- ½ tsp onion powder
- ½ tsp garlic salt
- ⅛ tsp black pepper
- ½ tsp mixed herbs

Directions:

1. Heat air fryer to 220°C
2. Beat the egg and egg white in a bowl
3. Sprinkle fish with herbs and spice mix, dip into the egg and then cover in the panko bread crumbs
4. Line air fryer basket with tin foil. Place the fish in the air fryer and coat with cooking spray
5. Cook for about 15 minutes until, fish is lightly browned

Garlic Tilapia

Servings: 2
Cooking Time:xx

Ingredients:

- 2 tilapia fillets
- 2 tsp chopped fresh chives
- 2 tsp chopped fresh parsley
- 2 tsp olive oil
- 1 tsp minced garlic
- Salt and pepper for seasoning

Directions:

1. Preheat the air fryer to 220°C
2. Take a small bowl and combine the olive oil with the chives, garlic, parsley and a little salt and pepper
3. Brush the mixture over the fish fillets
4. Place the fish into the air fryer and cook for 10 minutes, until flaky

Mushrooms Stuffed With Crab

Servings: 2
Cooking Time:xx

Ingredients:

- 500g large mushrooms
- 2 tsp salt
- Half a diced red onion
- 2 diced celery sticks
- 300g lump crab
- 35g seasoned breadcrumbs
- 1 egg
- 1 tsp oregano
- 1 tsp hot sauce
- 50g grated Parmesan cheese

Directions:

1. Preheat to 260°C
2. Take a baking sheet and arrange the mushrooms top down
3. Spray with a little cooking oil
4. Take a bowl and combine the onions, celery, breadcrumbs, egg, crab and half the cheese, oregano and hot sauce
5. Fill each mushroom with the mixture and make sure it's heaped over the top
6. Cover with the rest of the cheese
7. Place in the air fryer for 18 minutes

Parmesan-coated Fish Fingers

Servings: 2
Cooking Time:xx

Ingredients:

- 350 g/12 oz. cod loins
- 1 tablespoon grated Parmesan
- 40 g/½ cup dried breadcrumbs (gluten-free if you wish, see page 9)
- 1 egg, beaten
- 2 tablespoons plain/all-purpose flour (gluten free if you wish)

Directions:

1. Slice the cod into 6 equal fish fingers/sticks.
2. Mix the Parmesan together with the breadcrumbs. Lay out three bowls: one with flour, one with beaten egg and the other with the Parmesan breadcrumbs. Dip each fish finger/stick first into the flour, then the egg and then the breadcrumbs until fully coated.
3. Preheat the air-fryer to 180°C/350°F.
4. Add the fish to the preheated air-fryer and air-fry for 6 minutes. Check the internal temperature of the fish has reached at least 75°C/167°F using a meat thermometer – if not, cook for another few minutes. Serve immediately.

Thai Fish Cakes

Servings: 4
Cooking Time:xx
Ingredients:

- 200g pre-mashed potatoes
- 2 fillets of white fish, flaked and mashed
- 1 onion
- 1 tsp butter
- 1 tsp milk
- 1 lime zest and rind
- 3 tsp chilli
- 1 tsp Worcester sauce
- 1 tsp coriander
- 1 tsp mixed spice
- 1 tsp mixed herbs
- 50g breadcrumbs
- Salt and pepper to taste

Directions:

1. Cover the white fish in milk
2. in a mixing bowl place the fish and add the seasoning and mashed potatoes
3. Add the butter and remaining milk
4. Use your hands to create patties and place in the refrigerator for 3 hours
5. Preheat your air fryer to 200ºC
6. Cook for 15 minutes

Fish Taco Cauliflower Rice Bowls

Servings: 2
Cooking Time:xx
Ingredients:

- 400g fish of your choice, cut into strips
- 1 tsp chilli powder
- ½ tsp paprika
- 1 sliced avocado
- 25g pickled red onions
- 25g reduced fat sour cream
- ½ tsp cumin
- Salt and pepper to taste
- 300g cauliflower rice
- 1 tbsp lime juice
- 25g fresh coriander
- 1 tbsp sriracha

Directions:

1. Sprinkle both sides of the fish with chilli powder, cumin, paprika, salt and pepper

2. Heat the air fryer to 200ºC, cook the fish for about 12 minutes
3. cook the cauliflower rice according to instructions, mix in lime juice and coriander once cooked
4. Divide the cauliflower rice between two bowls, add the sliced avocado, fish and pickled red onions.
5. Mix the sour cream with the sriracha and drizzle over the top

Traditional Fish And Chips

Servings: 4
Cooking Time:xx
Ingredients:

- 4 potatoes, peeled and cut into chips
- 2 fish fillets of your choice
- 1 beaten egg
- 3 slices of wholemeal bread, grated into breadcrumbs
- 25g tortilla crisps
- 1 lemon rind and juice
- 1 tbsp parsley
- Salt and pepper to taste

Directions:

1. Preheat your air fryer to 200ºC
2. Place the chips inside and cook until crispy
3. Cut the fish fillets into 4 slices and season with lemon juice
4. Place the breadcrumbs, lemon rind, parsley, tortillas and seasoning into a food processor and blitz to create a crumb consistency
5. Place the breadcrumbs on a large plate
6. Coat the fish in the egg and then the breadcrumb mixture
7. Cook for 15 minutes at 180ºC

Air Fried Scallops

Servings: 2
Cooking Time:xx
Ingredients:

- 6 scallops
- 1 tbsp olive oil
- Salt and pepper to taste

Directions:

1. Brush the filets with olive oil
2. Sprinkle with salt and pepper
3. Place in the air fryer and cook at 200ºC for 2 mins

4. Turn the scallops over and cook for another 2 minutes

Gluten Free Honey And Garlic Shrimp

Servings: 2
Cooking Time:xx
Ingredients:
- 500g fresh shrimp
- 5 tbsp honey
- 2 tbsp gluten free soy sauce
- 2 tbsp tomato ketchup
- 250g frozen stir fry vegetables
- 1 crushed garlic clove
- 1 tsp fresh ginger
- 2 tbsp cornstarch

Directions:
1. Simmer the honey, soy sauce, garlic, tomato ketchup and ginger in a saucepan
2. Add the cornstarch and whisk until sauce thickens
3. Coat the shrimp with the sauce
4. Line the air fryer with foil and add the shrimp and vegetables
5. Cook at 180°C for 10 minutes

Peppery Lemon Shrimp

Servings: 2
Cooking Time:xx
Ingredients:
- 300g uncooked shrimp
- 1 tbsp olive oil
- 1 the juice of 1 lemon
- 0.25 tsp garlic powder
- 1 sliced lemon
- 1 tsp pepper
- 0.25 tsp paprika

Directions:
1. Heat the fryer to 200°C
2. Take a medium sized mixing bowl and combine the lemon juice, pepper, garlic powder, paprika and the olive oil together
3. Add the shrimp to the bowl and make sure they're well coated
4. Arrange the shrimp into the basket of the fryer
5. Cook for between 6-8 minutes, until firm and pink

Tilapia Fillets

Servings: 2
Cooking Time:xx
Ingredients:
- 2 tbsp melted butter
- 150g almond flour
- 3 tbsp mayonnaise
- 2tilapia fillets
- 25g thinly sliced almonds
- Salt and pepper to taste
- Vegetable oil spray

Directions:
1. Mix the almond flour, butter, pepper and salt together in a bowl
2. Spread mayonnaise on both sides of the fish
3. Cover the fillets in the almond flour mix
4. Spread one side of the fish with the sliced almonds
5. Spray the air fryer with the vegetable spray
6. Place in the air fryer and cook at 160°C for 10 minutes

Crispy Cajun Fish Fingers

Servings: 2
Cooking Time:xx
Ingredients:
- 350 g/12 oz. cod loins
- 1 teaspoon smoked paprika
- ½ teaspoon cayenne pepper
- ½ teaspoon onion granules
- ¾ teaspoon dried oregano
- ¼ teaspoon dried thyme
- ½ teaspoon salt
- ½ teaspoon unrefined sugar
- 40 g/½ cup dried breadcrumbs (gluten-free if you wish, see page 9)
- 2 tablespoons plain/all-purpose flour (gluten-free if you wish)
- 1 egg, beaten

Directions:
1. Slice the cod into 6 equal fish 'fingers'. Mix the spices, herbs, salt and sugar together, then combine with the breadcrumbs. Lay out three bowls: one with flour, one with beaten egg and one with the Cajun-spiced breadcrumbs. Dip each fish finger into the flour, then the egg, then the breadcrumbs until fully coated.
2. Preheat the air-fryer to 180°C/350°F.

3. Add the fish to the preheated air-fryer and air-fry for 6 minutes, until cooked inside. Check the internal temperature of the fish has reached at least 75°C/167°F using a meat thermometer – if not, cook for another few minutes.

Crunchy Fish

Servings: 4
Cooking Time:xx
Ingredients:
- 200g dry breadcrumbs
- 4 tbsp olive oil
- 4 fillets of white fish
- 1 beaten egg
- 1 sliced lemon

Directions:
1. Heat the fryer to 180°C
2. In a medium mixing bowl, combine the olive oil and the breadcrumbs
3. Take the fish and first dip it into the egg and then the breadcrumbs, making sure they are evenly coated well
4. Arrange the fish into the basket
5. Cook for 12 minutes
6. Remove and serve with lemon slices

Mahi Fish Tacos

Servings: 4
Cooking Time:xx
Ingredients:
- 400g fresh mahi
- 8 small corn tortillas
- 2 tsp cajun seasoning
- 5 tbsp sour cream
- 2 tbsp mayonnaise
- 2 tbsp scotch bonnet pepper sauce (use 1 tbsp if you don't like your food too spicy)
- 1 tbsp sriracha sauce
- 2 tbsp lime juice
- Salt and pepper to taste
- 1 tbsp vegetable oil

Directions:
1. Clean the mahi. Cut into half inch slices and season with salt

2. Mix quarter parts cayenne pepper and black pepper with cajun seasoning. Sprinkle onto fish
3. Brush pepper sauce on both sides of the fish
4. Set the air fryer to 180°C and cook for about 10 minutes or until golden brown
5. Whilst the fish cooks make the chipotle lime cream. Mix the mayo, sour cream, lime juice sriracha and cayenne pepper
6. Assemble tacos and enjoy

Zesty Fish Fillets

Servings: 2
Cooking Time:xx
Ingredients:
- 30g dry ranch seasoning
- 2 beaten eggs
- 100g breadcrumbs
- 2.5 tbsp vegetable oil
- 4 fish fillets of your choice
- Wedges of lemon to serve

Directions:
1. Preheat the air fryer to 180°C
2. Mix the bread crumbs and seasoning together add the oil and combine
3. Dip the fish into the egg and then coat in the breadcrumb mix
4. Place in the air fryer and cook for 12 minutes
5. Serve with lemon wedges

Crispy Nacho Prawns

Servings: 6
Cooking Time:xx
Ingredients:
- 1 egg
- 18 large prawns
- 1 bag of nacho cheese flavoured corn chips, crushed

Directions:
1. Wash the prawns and pat dry
2. Place the chips into a bowl
3. In another bowl, whisk the egg
4. Dip the prawns into the egg and then the nachos
5. Preheat the air fryer to 180°C
6. Cook for 8 minutes

Beef & Lamb And Pork Recipes

Chinese Pork With Pineapple

Servings: 4
Cooking Time:xx
Ingredients:

- 450g pork loin, cubed
- ½ tsp salt
- ½ tsp pepper
- 1 tbsp brown sugar
- 75g fresh coriander, chopped
- 2 tbsp toasted sesame seeds
- ½ pineapple, cubed
- 1 sliced red pepper
- 1 minced clove of garlic
- 1 tsp ginger
- 2 tbsp soy
- 1 tbsp oil

Directions:

1. Season the pork with salt and pepper
2. Add all ingredients to the air fryer
3. Cook at 180°C for 17 minutes
4. Serve and garnish with coriander and toasted sesame seeds

Pork Chops With Sprouts

Servings: 2
Cooking Time:xx
Ingredients:

- 300g pork chops
- ⅛ tsp salt
- ½ tsp pepper
- 250g Brussels sprouts quartered
- 1 tsp olive oil
- 1 tsp maple syrup
- 1 tsp dijon mustard

Directions:

1. Season the pork chops with salt and pepper
2. Mix together oil, maple syrup and mustard. Add Brussels sprouts
3. Add pork chops and Brussels sprouts to the air fryer and cook at 200°C for about 10 minutes

Cheese & Ham Sliders

Servings: 4
Cooking Time:xx
Ingredients:

- 8 slider bread rolls, cut in half
- 16 slices of sweet ham
- 16 slices of Swiss cheese
- 5 tbsp mayonnaise
- 1/2 tsp paprika
- 1 tsp onion powder
- 1 tsp dill

Directions:

1. Place 2 slices of ham into each bread roll and 2 slices of cheese
2. Take a bowl and combine the mayonnaise with the onion powder, dill and paprika
3. Add half a tablespoon of the sauce on top of each piece of cheese
4. Place the top on the bread slider
5. Cook at 220°C for 5 minutes

Asparagus & Steak Parcels

Servings: 4
Cooking Time:xx
Ingredients:

- 500g flank steak, cut into 6 equal pieces
- 75ml Tamari sauce
- 2 crushed garlic cloves
- 250g trimmed asparagus
- 3 large bell peppers, thinly sliced
- 2 tbsp butter
- Salt and pepper to taste

Directions:

1. Season the steak to your liking
2. Place the meat in a zip top bag and add the Tamari and garlic, sealing the bag closed
3. Make sure the steaks are fully coated in the sauce and leave them in the fright at least 1 hour, but preferably overnight
4. Remove the steaks from the bag and throw the marinade away
5. Place the peppers and sliced asparagus in the centre of each steak piece
6. Roll the steak up and secure in place with a tooth pick
7. Preheat your air fryer to 250°C

8. Transfer the meat parcels to the air fryer and cook for 5 minutes
9. Allow to rest before serving
10. Melt the butter in a saucepan, over a medium heat, adding the juices from the air fryer
11. Combine well and keep cooking until thickened
12. Pour the sauce over the steak parcels and season to your liking

Cheesy Meatball Sub

Servings: 2
Cooking Time:xx
Ingredients:
- 8 frozen pork meatballs
- 5 tbsp marinara sauce
- 160g grated parmesan cheese
- 2 sub rolls or hotdog rolls
- 1/4 tsp dried oregano

Directions:
1. Preheat the air fryer to 220ºC
2. Place the meatball in the air fryer and cook for around 10 minutes, turning halfway through
3. Place the marinara sauce in a bowl
4. Add the meatballs to the sauce and coat completely
5. Add the oregano on top and coat once more
6. Take the bread roll and add the mixture inside
7. Top with the cheese
8. Place the meatball sub back in the air fryer and cook for 2 minutes until the bad is toasted and the cheese has melted

Sweet And Sticky Ribs

Servings:2
Cooking Time:1 Hour 15 Minutes
Ingredients:
- 500 g / 17.6 oz pork ribs
- 2 cloves garlic, minced
- 2 tbsp soy sauce
- 2 tsp honey
- 1 tbsp cayenne pepper
- 1 tsp olive oil
- 2 tbsp BBQ sauce
- 1 tsp salt
- 1 tsp black pepper

Directions:
1. Place the pork ribs on a clean surface and cut them into smaller chunks if necessary.

2. In a small mixing bowl, combine the minced garlic, soy sauce, 1 tsp honey, cayenne pepper, olive oil, BBQ sauce, salt, and pepper. Rub the pork ribs into the sauce and spice the mixture until fully coated.
3. Place the coated ribs in the fridge for 1 hour. Meanwhile, preheat the air fryer to 180 °C / 350 °F and line the bottom of the basket with parchment paper.
4. After one hour, transfer the pork ribs into the prepared air fryer basket. Close the lid and cook for 15 minutes, using tongs to turn them halfway through.
5. Once cooked, remove the ribs from the air fryer and use a brush to top each rib with the remaining 1 tsp honey.
6. Return the ribs to the air fryer for a further 2-3 minutes to heat the honey glaze before serving.

Fillet Mignon Wrapped In Bacon

Servings: 2
Cooking Time:xx
Ingredients:
- 1 kg filet mignon
- 500g bacon slices
- Olive oil

Directions:
1. Wrap the fillets in bacon
2. Season with salt and pepper and brush with olive oil
3. Place in the air fryer cook at 200ºC for 9 minutes turning halfway through

Pizza Dogs

Servings: 2
Cooking Time:xx
Ingredients:
- 2 pork hot dogs
- 4 pepperoni slices, halved
- 150g pizza sauce
- 2 hotdog buns
- 75g grated cheese
- 2 tsp sliced olives

Directions:
1. Preheat air fryer to 190ºC
2. Place 4 slits down each hotdog, place in the air fryer and cook for 3 minutes

3. Place a piece of pepperoni into each slit, add pizza sauce to hot dog buns
4. Place hotdogs in the buns and top with cheese and olives
5. Cook in the air fryer for about 2 minutes

Lamb Burgers

Servings: 4
Cooking Time:xx
Ingredients:

- 600g minced lamb
- 2 tsp garlic puree
- 1 tsp harissa paste
- 2 tbsp Moroccan spice
- Salt and pepper

Directions:

1. Place all the ingredients in a bowl and mix well
2. Form into patties
3. Place in the air fryer and cook at 180°C for 18 minutes

Traditional Empanadas

Servings: 2
Cooking Time:xx
Ingredients:

- 300g minced beef
- 1 tbsp olive oil
- ¼ cup finely chopped onion
- 150g chopped mushrooms
- ⅛ tsp cinnamon
- 4 chopped tomatoes
- 2 tsp chopped garlic
- 6 green olives
- ¼ tsp paprika
- ¼ tsp cumin
- 8 goyoza wrappers
- 1 beaten egg

Directions:

1. Heat oil in a pan add onion and minced beef and cook until browned
2. Add mushrooms and cook for 6 minutes
3. Add garlic, olives, paprika, cumin and cinnamon, and cook for about 3 minutes
4. Stir in tomatoes and cook for 1 minute, set aside allow to cool
5. Place 1 ½ tbsp of filling in each goyoza wrapper
6. Brush edges with egg fold over and seal pinching edges

7. Place in the air fryer and cook at 200 for about 7 minutes

Parmesan Crusted Pork Chops

Servings: 6
Cooking Time:xx
Ingredients:

- 6 pork chops
- ½ tsp salt
- ¼ tsp pepper
- 1 tsp paprika
- 3 tbsp parmesan
- ½ tsp onion powder
- ¼ tsp chilli powder
- 2 eggs beaten
- 250g pork rind crumbs

Directions:

1. Preheat the air fryer to 200°C
2. Season the pork with the seasonings
3. Place the pork rind into a food processor and blend into crumbs
4. Mix the pork rind and seasonings in a bowl
5. Beat the eggs in a separate bowl
6. Dip the pork into the egg then into the crumb mix
7. Place pork in the air fryer and cook for about 15 minutes until crispy

Italian Meatballs

Servings: 12
Cooking Time:xx
Ingredients:

- 2 tbsp olive oil
- 2 tbsp minced shallot
- 3 cloves garlic minced
- 100g panko crumbs
- 35g chopped parsley
- 1 tbsp chopped rosemary
- 60ml milk
- 400g minced pork
- 250g turkey sausage
- 1 egg beaten
- 1 tbsp dijon mustard
- 1 tbsp finely chopped thyme

Directions:

1. Preheat air fryer to 200°C
2. Heat oil in a pan and cook the garlic and shallot over a medium heat for 1-2 minutes

3. Mix the panko and milk in a bowl and allow to stand for 5 minutes
4. Add all the ingredients to the panko mix and combine well
5. Shape into 1 ½ inch meatballs and cook for 12 minutes

Beef Nacho Pinwheels

Servings: 6
Cooking Time:xx
Ingredients:

- 500g minced beef
- 1 packet of taco seasoning
- 300ml water
- 300ml sour cream
- 6 tostadas
- 6 flour tortillas
- 3 tomatoes
- 250g nacho cheese
- 250g shredded lettuce
- 250g Mexican cheese

Directions:

1. Preheat air fryer to 200°C
2. Brown the mince in a pan and add the taco seasoning
3. Share the remaining ingredients between the tortillas
4. Fold the edges of the tortillas up towards the centre, should look like a pinwheel
5. Lay seam down in the air fryer and cook for 2 minutes
6. Turnover and cook for a further 2 minutes

Roast Beef

Servings: 2
Cooking Time:xx
Ingredients:

- 400g beef fillet
- 1 tbsp olive oil
- 1 tsp salt
- 1 tsp rosemary

Directions:

1. Preheat the air fryer to 180°C
2. Mix salt, rosemary and oil on a plate
3. Coat the beef with the mix
4. Place the beef in the air fryer and cook for 45 minutes turning halfway

Chinese Chilli Beef

Servings: 2
Cooking Time:xx
Ingredients:

- 4 tbsp light soy sauce
- 1 tsp honey
- 3 tbsp tomato ketchup
- 1 tsp Chinese 5 spice
- 1 tbsp oil
- 6 tbsp sweet chilli sauce
- 1 tbsp lemon juice
- 400g frying steak
- 2 tbsp cornflour

Directions:

1. Slice the steak into strips, put into a bowl and cover with cornflour and 5 spice
2. Add to the air fryer and cook for 6 minutes at 200°C
3. Whilst the beef is cooking mix together the remaining ingredients
4. Add to the air fryer and cook for another 3 minutes

Meatballs In Tomato Sauce

Servings: 4
Cooking Time:xx
Ingredients:

- 1 small onion
- 300g minced pork
- 1 tbsp chopped parsley
- 1 tbsp thyme
- 1 egg
- 3 tbsp bread crumbs
- Salt and pepper to taste

Directions:

1. Place all ingredients into a bowl and mix well
2. Shape mixture into 12 meatballs
3. Heat the air fryer to 200°C
4. Place the meatballs into the air fryer and cook for about 7 minutes
5. Tip the meatballs into an oven dish add the tomato sauce and cook for about 5 minutes in the air fryer until warmed through

Pork Taquitos

Servings: 5
Cooking Time:xx
Ingredients:

- 400g shredded pork
- 500g grated mozzarella
- 10 flour tortillas
- The juice of 1 lime
- Cooking spray

Directions:

1. Preheat air fryer to 190ºC
2. Sprinkle lime juice on the pork and mix
3. Microwave tortilla for about 10 seconds to soften
4. Add a little pork and cheese to a tortilla
5. Roll then tortilla up, and place in the air fryer
6. Cook for about 7 minutes until golden, turn halfway through cooking

Hamburgers With Feta

Servings: 4
Cooking Time:xx
Ingredients:

- 400g minced beef
- 250g crumbled feta
- 25g chopped green olives
- ½ tsp garlic powder
- ½ cup chopped onion
- 2 tbsp Worcestershire sauce
- ½ tsp steak seasoning
- Salt to taste

Directions:

1. Mix all the ingredients in a bowl
2. Divide the mix into four and shape into patties
3. Place in the air fryer and cook at 200ºC for about 15 minutes

Butter Steak & Asparagus

Servings: 6
Cooking Time:xx
Ingredients:

- 500g steak, cut into 6 pieces
- Salt and pepper
- 75g tamari sauce
- 2 cloves crushed garlic
- 400g asparagus
- 3 sliced peppers
- 25g balsamic vinegar
- 50g beef broth
- 2 tbsp butter

Directions:

1. Season steaks with salt and pepper
2. Place steaks in a bowl, add tamari sauce and garlic make sure steaks are covered, leave to marinate for at least 1hr
3. Place steaks on a board, fill with peppers and asparagus, roll the steak around and secure with tooth picks
4. Set your fryer to 200ºC and cook for 5 minutes.
5. Whilst cooking heat the broth, butter and balsamic vinegar in a saucepan until thickened
6. Pour over the steaks and serve

Pork With Chinese 5 Spice

Servings: 4
Cooking Time:xx
Ingredients:

- 2 pork rounds cut into chunks
- 2 large eggs
- 1 tsp sesame oil
- 200g cornstarch
- 1/4 tsp salt
- ½ tsp pepper
- 3 tbsp canola oil
- 1 tsp Chinese 5 spice

Directions:

1. In a bowl mix the corn starch, salt, pepper and 5 spice
2. Mix the eggs and sesame oil in another bowl
3. Dip the pork into the egg and then cover in the corn starch mix
4. Place in the air fryer and cook at 170ºC for 11-12 minutes, shaking halfway through
5. Serve with sweet and sour sauce

Jamaican Jerk Pork

Servings: 4
Cooking Time:xx
Ingredients:

- 400g pork butt cut into 3 pieces
- 100g jerk paste

Directions:

1. Rub the pork with jerk paste and marinate for 4 hours
2. Preheat air fryer to 190ºC
3. Place pork in the air fryer and cook for about 20 minutes turning halfway

Beef Stuffed Peppers

Servings: 4
Cooking Time:xx
Ingredients:

- 4 bell peppers
- ½ chopped onion
- 1 minced garlic clove
- 500g minced beef
- 5 tbsp tomato sauce
- 100g grated cheese
- 2 tsp Worcestershire sauce
- 1 tsp garlic powder
- A pinch of black pepper
- ½ tsp chilli powder
- 1 tsp dried basil
- 75g cooked rice

Directions:

1. Cook the onions, minced beef, garlic and all the seasonings until the meat is browned
2. Remove from the heat and add Worcestershire sauce, rice, ½ the cheese and ⅔ of the tomato sauce mix well
3. Cut the tops off the peppers and remove the seeds
4. Stuff the peppers with the mixture and place in the air fryer
5. Cook at 200°C for about 11 minutes
6. When there are 3 minutes remaining top the peppers with the rest of the tomato sauce and cheese

Breaded Pork Chops

Servings: 6
Cooking Time:xx
Ingredients:

- 6 boneless pork chops
- 1 beaten egg
- 100g panko crumbs
- 75g crushed cornflakes
- 2 tbsp parmesan
- 1 ¼ tsp paprika
- ½ tsp garlic powder
- ½ tsp onion powder
- ¼ tsp chilli powder
- Salt and pepper to taste

Directions:

1. Heat the air fryer to 200°C
2. Season the pork chops with salt

3. Mix the panko, cornflakes, salt, parmesan, garlic powder, onion powder, paprika, chilli powder and pepper in a bowl
4. Beat the egg in another bowl
5. Dip the pork in the egg and then coat with panko mix
6. Place in the air fryer and cook for about 12 minutes turning halfway

Tender Ham Steaks

Servings: 1
Cooking Time:xx
Ingredients:

- 1 ham steak
- 2 tbsp brown sugar
- 1 tsp honey
- 2 tbsp melted butter

Directions:

1. Preheat the air fryer to 220°C
2. Combine the melted butter and brown sugar until smooth
3. Add the ham to the air fryer and brush both sides with the butter mixture
4. Cook for 12 minutes, turning halfway through and re-brushing the ham
5. Drizzle honey on top before serving

Beef Fried Rice

Servings: 2
Cooking Time:xx
Ingredients:

- 400g cooked rice
- 250g cooked beef strips
- 1 tbsp sesame oil
- 1 diced onion
- 1 egg
- 2 tsp garlic powder
- Salt and pepper
- 1 tbsp vegetable oil
- 250g frozen peas

Directions:

1. Preheat air fryer to 175°C
2. Season the beef with salt, pepper and garlic powder, cook in a pan until about ¾ cooked
3. Mix the rice with peas carrots and vegetable oil, add the beef and mix
4. Add to the air fryer and cook for about 10 minutes
5. Add the egg and cook until the egg is done

Vegetable & Beef Frittata

Servings: 2
Cooking Time:xx
Ingredients:

- 250g ground beef
- 4 shredded hash browns
- 8 eggs
- Half a diced onion
- 1 courgette, diced
- 250g grated cheese
- Salt and pepper for seasoning

Directions:

1. Break the ground beef up and place in the air fryer
2. Add the onion and combine well
3. Cook at 260ºC for 3 minutes
4. Stir the mixture and cook foremother 2 minutes
5. Remove and clean the tray
6. Add the courgette to the air fryer and spray with a little cooking oil
7. Cook for 3 minutes
8. Add to the meat mixture and combine
9. Take a mixing bowl and combine the cheese, has browns, and eggs
10. Add the meat and courgette to the bowl and season with salt and pepper
11. Take a 6" round baking tray and add the mixture
12. Cook for 8 minutes before cutting lines in the top and cooking for another 8 minutes
13. Cut into slices before serving

Breaded Bone-in Pork Chops

Servings: 2
Cooking Time:xx
Ingredients:

- 2 pork chops with the bone in
- 250g Italian breadcrumbs
- 2 tbsp mayonnaise
- 1/2 tsp garlic powder
- 1/2 tsp onion powder
- 1/2 tsp thyme
- 1/2 tsp paprika
- Salt and pepper to taste

Directions:

1. Preheat the air fryer to 260ºC
2. Take a large bowl and add the breadcrumbs, garlic powder, paprika, salt and pepper, and thyme, and onion powder, combining well
3. Cover the pork chops with the mayonnaise making sure to cover both sides
4. Coat the meat with the seasoning mixture, making sure it is fully covered
5. Cook the pork chops in the fryer for 10 minutes, turning over halfway

Cheesy Beef Enchiladas

Servings: 4
Cooking Time:xx
Ingredients:

- 500g minced beef
- 1 packet taco seasoning
- 8 tortillas
- 300g grated cheese
- 150g soured cream
- 1 can black beans
- 1 can chopped tomatoes
- 1 can mild chopped chillies
- 1 can red enchilada sauce
- 300g chopped coriander

Directions:

1. Brown the beef and add the taco seasoning
2. Add the beef, beans, tomatoes and chillies to the tortillas
3. Line the air fryer with foil and put the tortillas in
4. Pour the enchilada sauce over the top and sprinkle with cheese
5. Cook at 200ºC for five minutes, remove from air fryer add toppings and serve

Bbq Ribs

Servings: 2
Cooking Time:xx
Ingredients:

- 500g ribs
- 3 chopped garlic cloves
- 4 tbsp bbq sauce
- 1 tbsp honey
- ½ tsp five spice
- 1 tsp sesame oil
- 1 tsp salt
- 1 tsp black pepper
- 1 tsp soy sauce

Directions:

1. Chop the ribs into small pieces and place them in a bowl
2. Add all the ingredients into the bowl and mix well
3. Marinate for 4 hours
4. Preheat the air fryer to 180°C
5. Place the ribs into the air fryer and cook for 15 minutes
6. Coat the ribs in honey and cook for a further 15 minutes

Mustard Glazed Pork

Servings: 4
Cooking Time:xx
Ingredients:

- 500g pork tenderloin
- 1 tbsp minced garlic
- ¼ tsp salt
- ⅛ tsp cracked black pepper
- 75g yellow mustard
- 3 tbsp brown sugar
- 1 tsp Italian seasoning
- 1 tsp rosemary

Directions:

1. Cut slits into the pork place the minced garlic into the slits, season with the salt and pepper
2. Add the remaining ingredients to a bowl and whisk to combine
3. Rub the mix over the pork and allow to marinate for 2 hours
4. Place in the air fryer and cook at 200°C for 20 minutes

Mongolian Beef

Servings: 4
Cooking Time:xx
Ingredients:

- 500g steak
- 25g cornstarch
- 2 tsp vegetable oil
- ½ tsp ginger
- 1 tbsp garlic minced
- 75g soy sauce
- 75g water
- 100g brown sugar

Directions:

1. Slice the steak and coat in corn starch
2. Place in the air fryer and cook at 200°C for 10 minutes turning halfway

3. Place remaining ingredients in a sauce pan and gently warm
4. When cooked place the steak in a bowl and pour the sauce over

Salt And Pepper Belly Pork

Servings: 4
Cooking Time:xx
Ingredients:

- 500g belly pork
- 1 tsp pepper
- ½ tsp salt

Directions:

1. Cut the pork into bite size pieces and season with salt and pepper
2. Heat the air fryer to 200°C
3. Place in the air fryer and cook for 15 minutes until crisp

Sticky Asian Beef

Servings: 2
Cooking Time:xx
Ingredients:

- 1 tbsp coconut oil
- 2 sliced peppers
- 25g liquid aminos
- 25g cup water
- 100g brown sugar
- ¼ tsp pepper
- ½ tsp ground ginger
- ½ tbsp minced garlic
- 1 tsp red pepper flakes
- 600g steak thinly sliced
- ¼ tsp salt

Directions:

1. Melt the coconut oil in a pan, add the peppers and cook until softened
2. In another pan add the aminos, brown sugar, ginger, garlic and pepper flakes. Mix and bring to the boil, simmer for 10 mins
3. Season the steak with salt and pepper
4. Put the steak in the air fryer and cook at 200°C for 10 minutes. Turn the steak and cook for a further 5 minutes until crispy
5. Add the steak to the peppers then mix with the sauce
6. Serve with rice

Pulled Pork, Bacon, And Cheese Sliders

Servings:2
Cooking Time:30 Minutes
Ingredients:

- 2 x 50 g / 3.5 oz pork steaks
- 1 tsp salt
- 1 tsp black pepper
- 4 slices bacon strips, chopped into small pieces
- 1 tbsp soy sauce
- 1 tbsp BBQ sauce
- 100 g / 7 oz cheddar cheese, grated
- 2 bread buns

Directions:

1. Preheat the air fryer to 200 °C / 400 °F and line the bottom of the basket with parchment paper.
2. Place the pork steaks on a clean surface and season with salt and black pepper. Move the pork steak in the prepared air fryer basket and cook for 15 minutes.
3. Remove the steak from the air fryer and shred using two forks. Mix with the chopped bacon in a heatproof bowl and place the bowl in the air fryer. Cook for 10 minutes.
4. Remove the bowl from the air fryer and stir in the soy sauce and BBQ sauce. Return the bowl to the air fryer basket and continue cooking for a further 5 minutes.
5. Meanwhile, spread the cheese across one half of the bread buns. Top with the cooked pulled pork and an extra squirt of BBQ sauce.

Beef Kebobs

Servings: 4
Cooking Time:xx
Ingredients:

- 500g cubed beef
- 25g low fat sour cream
- 2 tbsp soy sauce
- 8 x 6 inch skewers
- 1 bell pepper
- Half an onion

Directions:

1. Mix the sour cream and soy sauce in a bowl, add the cubed beef and marinate for at least 30 minutes
2. Cut the pepper and onion into 1 inch pieces, soak the skewers in water for 10 minutes
3. Thread beef, bell peppers and onion onto skewers
4. Cook in the air fryer at 200°C for 10 minutes turning halfway

Japanese Pork Chops

Servings: 4
Cooking Time:xx
Ingredients:

- 6 boneless pork chops
- 30g flour
- 2 beaten eggs
- 2 tbsp sweet chilli sauce
- 500g cup seasoned breadcrumbs
- ⅛ tsp salt
- ⅛ tsp pepper
- Tonkatsu sauce to taste

Directions:

1. Place the flour, breadcrumbs and eggs in 3 separate bowls
2. Sprinkle both sides of the pork with salt and pepper
3. Coat the pork in flour, egg and then breadcrumbs
4. Place in the air fryer and cook at 180°C for 8 minutes, turn then cook for a further 5 minutes
5. Serve with sauces on the side

Char Siu Buffalo

Servings: 2
Cooking Time:xx
Ingredients:

- 1 kg beef, cut into strips
- 4 tbsp honey
- 2 tbsp sugar
- 2 tbsp char siu sauce
- 2 tbsp oyster sauce
- 2 tbsp soy sauce
- 2 tbsp olive oil
- 2 tsp minced garlic
- ¼ tsp bi carbonate of soda

Directions:

1. Place all the ingredients in a bowl, mix well and marinate over night
2. Line the air fryer with foil, add the beef, keep the marinade to one side
3. Cook at 200°C for 10 minutes

4. Brush the pork with the sauce and cook for another 20 minutes at 160ºC
5. Remove the meat and set aside
6. Strain the marinade into a saucepan, heat until it thickens
7. Drizzle over the pork and serve with rice

Taco Lasagne Pie

Servings: 4
Cooking Time:xx
Ingredients:

- 450g ground beef
- 2 tbsp olive oil
- 1 chopped onion
- 1 minced garlic clove
- 1 tsp cumin
- 1 tsp oregano
- 1/2 tsp adobo
- 266g grated Cheddar cheese
- 4 flour tortillas
- 112g tomato sauce

Directions:

1. Soften the onions with the olive oil in a frying pan
2. Add the beef and garlic until the meat has browned
3. Add the tomato sauce, cumin, oregano, and adobo and combine
4. Allow to simmer for a few minutes
5. Place one tortilla on the bottom of your air fryer basket
6. Add a meat layer, followed by a layer of the cheese, and continue alternating this routine until you have no meat left
7. Add a tortilla on top and sprinkle with the rest of the cheese
8. Cook at 180ºC for 8 minutes

Kheema Meatloaf

Servings: 4
Cooking Time:xx
Ingredients:

- 500g minced beef
- 2 eggs
- 1 diced onion
- 200g sliced coriander
- 1 tbsp minced ginger
- ⅛ cardamom pod
- 1 tbsp minced garlic

- 2 tsp garam masala
- 1 tsp salt
- 1 tsp cayenne
- 1 tsp turmeric
- ½ tsp cinnamon

Directions:

1. Place all the ingredients in a large bowl and mix well
2. Place meat in an 8 inch pan and set air fryer to 180ºC
3. Place in the air fryer and cook for 15 minutes
4. Slice and serve

Crispy Chili Sausages

Servings:4
Cooking Time:20 Minutes
Ingredients:

- 8 sausages, uncooked
- 2 eggs
- ½ tsp salt
- ½ black pepper
- ½ tsp chili flakes
- ½ tsp paprika

Directions:

1. Preheat the air fryer to 180 ºC / 350 ºF and line the bottom of the basket with parchment paper.
2. Place the sausages in the air fryer and cook for 5 minutes until slightly browned, but not fully cooked. Remove from the air fryer and set aside.
3. While the sausages are cooking, whisk together the eggs, salt, black pepper, chili flakes, and paprika. Coat the sausages evenly in the egg and spice mixture.
4. Return the sausages to the air fryer and cook for a further 5 minutes until brown and crispy.
5. Eat the sausages while hot with a side of steamed vegetables or place them in a sandwich for lunch.

Beef Wellington

Servings: 4
Cooking Time:xx
Ingredients:

- 300g chicken liver pate
- 500g shortcrust pastry
- 600g beef fillet
- 1 egg beaten
- Salt and pepper

Directions:

1. Remove all the visible fat from the beef season with salt and pepper. Wrap in cling film and place in the fridge for 1 hour
2. Roll out the pastry, brush the edges with egg
3. Spread the pate over the pastry. Remove the clingfilm from the beef and place in the center of the pastry
4. Seal the pastry around the meat
5. Place in the air fryer and cook at 160ºC for 35 minutes

German Rouladen

Servings: 2
Cooking Time:xx
Ingredients:

- 2 tbsp oil
- 2 cups sliced onion
- 4 tbsp sour cream
- 1 tbsp tomato paste
- 1 tsp chopped parsley
- 400g steak
- ¼ cup dijon mustard
- 4 bacon strips

Directions:

1. Add salt and pepper to the onions and mix
2. Cook the onions in the air fryer at 200ºC for 5-6 minutes
3. Put half the onions in a bowl and mix with sour cream, 2 tsp parsley and tomato paste
4. Spread the mustard on to the steak then add the bacon and onion
5. Roll the steak up tightly and cook in the air fryer for 8-10 minutes

Steak Fajitas

Servings: 4
Cooking Time:xx
Ingredients:

- 500g sliced steak
- 25g pineapple juice
- 2 tbsp lime juice
- 1 tbsp olive oil
- 1 tbsp soy sauce
- 1 tbsp minced garlic
- ½ tbsp chilli powder
- 1/2 tsp paprika
- 1 tsp cumin
- 1 pepper
- 1 onion
- Salt and pepper to taste

Directions:

1. Mix pineapple juice, lime juice, olive oil, soy sauce, garlic, cumin chilli powder and paprika. Pour over the steak and marinate for 4 hours
2. Line the air fryer with foil, add the peppers and onions, season with salt and pepper
3. Cook at 200ºC for 10 minutes, add the steak and cook for another 7 minutes
4. Serve with tortillas
5. Set your fryer to 170ºC and cook the sandwich for 4 minutes
6. Turn the sandwich over and cook for another 3 minutes
7. Turn the sandwich out and serve whilst hot
8. Repeat with the other remaining sandwich

Roast Pork

Servings: 4
Cooking Time:xx
Ingredients:

- 500g pork joint
- 1 tbsp olive oil
- 1 tsp salt

Directions:

1. Preheat air fryer to 180ºC
2. Score the pork skin with a knife
3. Drizzle the pork with oil and rub it into the skin, sprinkle with salt
4. Place in the air fryer and cook for about 50 minutes

Pork Chops With Raspberry And Balsamic

Servings: 4
Cooking Time:xx
Ingredients:

- 2 large eggs
- 30ml milk
- 250g panko bread crumbs
- 250g finely chopped pecans
- 1 tbsp orange juice
- 4 pork chops
- 30ml balsamic vinegar
- 2 tbsp brown sugar
- 2 tbsp raspberry jam

Directions:

1. Preheat air fryer to 200°C
2. Mix the eggs and milk together in a bowl
3. In another bowl mix the breadcrumbs and pecans
4. Coat the pork chops in flour, egg and then coat in the breadcrumbs
5. Place in the air fryer and cook for 12 minutes until golden turning halfway
6. Put the remaining ingredients in a pan simmer for about 6 minutes, serve with the pork chops

Sausage Burritos

Servings:4
Cooking Time:20 Minutes
Ingredients:

- 1 medium sweet potato
- 2 tbsp olive oil
- 1 tsp salt
- 1 tsp black pepper
- 8 sausages, uncooked
- 4 white flour tortillas
- 4 eggs, beaten
- 200 ml milk (any kind)
- 100 g / 3.5 oz cheddar cheese, grated

Directions:

1. Preheat the air fryer to 200 °C / 400 °F and line the air fryer mesh basket with parchment paper.
2. Peel the sweet potato and cut it into small chunks.
3. Place the sweet potato chunks in a bowl and toss in 1 tbsp olive oil. Sprinkle salt and pepper over the top.
4. Transfer the sweet potato chunks into the air fryer and cook for 8-10 minutes until hot. Remove from the air fryer and set aside to drain on paper towels.
5. Heat 1 tbsp olive oil in a medium frying pan and cook the sausages for 5-7 minutes until slightly browned. Remove the sausages and set them aside on paper towels to drain.
6. In a bowl, whisk together the beaten eggs and milk, and pour into the hot frying pan. Cook the eggs and use a fork to scramble them as they cook in the pan.
7. Once the eggs are cooked, mix them with the potatoes, sausages, and cheddar cheese in a bowl.
8. Spread the mixture evenly across the 4 white flour tortillas and roll them each up into tight burritos. Use a toothpick to keep them together if necessary.
9. Place the burritos into the hot air fryer and cook for 6-8 minutes, turning them over halfway through.
10. Enjoy the burritos for breakfast or lunch.

Tahini Beef Bites

Servings: 2
Cooking Time:xx
Ingredients:

- 500g sirloin steak, cut into cubes
- 2 tbsp Za'atar seasoning
- 1 tsp olive oil
- 25g Tahini
- 25g warm water
- 1 tbsp lemon juice
- 1 clove of garlic
- Salt to taste

Directions:

1. Preheat the air fryer to 250°C
2. Take a bowl and combine the oil with the steak, salt, and Za'atar seasoning
3. Place in the air fryer and cook for 10 minutes, turning halfway through
4. Take a bowl and combine the water, garlic, lemon juice, salt, and tahini, or use a food processor if you have one
5. Pour the sauce over the bites and serve

Pork Schnitzel

Servings: 2
Cooking Time:xx
Ingredients:

- 3 pork steaks, cut into cubes
- Salt and pepper
- 175g flour
- 2 eggs
- 175g breadcrumbs

Directions:

1. Sprinkle the pork with salt and pepper
2. Coat in the flour then dip in the egg
3. Coat the pork in breadcrumbs
4. Place in the air fryer and cook at 175°C for 20 minutes turning halfway
5. Serve with red cabbage

Air Fryer Pork Bratwurst

Servings: 2
Cooking Time:xx
Ingredients:

- 2 pork bratwursts
- 2 hotdog bread rolls
- 2 tbsp tomato sauce

Directions:

1. Preheat the air fryer to 200°C
2. Place the bratwurst in the fryer and cook for 10 minutes, turning halfway
3. Remove and place in the open bread rolls
4. Place back into the air fryer for 1 to 2 minutes, until the read is slightly crisped
5. Enjoy with the tomato sauce either on top or on the side

Meatloaf

Servings: 2
Cooking Time:xx
Ingredients:

- 500g minced pork
- 1 egg
- 3 tbsp breadcrumbs
- 2 mushrooms thickly sliced
- 1 tbsp olive oil
- 1 chopped onion
- 1 tbsp chopped thyme
- 1 tsp salt
- Ground black pepper

Directions:

1. Preheat air fryer to 200°C
2. Combine all the ingredients in a bowl
3. Put the mix into a pan and press down firmly, coat with olive oil
4. Place pan in the air fryer and cook for 25 minutes

Poultry Recipes

Turkey Cutlets In Mushroom Sauce

Servings: 2
Cooking Time:xx
Ingredients:

- 2 turkey cutlets
- 1 tbsp butter
- 1 can of cream of mushroom sauce
- 160ml milk
- Salt and pepper for seasoning

Directions:

1. Preheat the air fryer to 220°C
2. Brush the turkey cults with the butter and seasoning
3. Place in the air fryer and cook for 11 minutes
4. Add the mushroom soup and milk to a pan and cook over the stone for around 10 minutes, stirring every so often
5. Top the turkey cutlets with the sauce

Thai Turkey Burgers

Servings: 4
Cooking Time:xx
Ingredients:

- 1 courgette/zucchini, about 200 g/7 oz.
- 400 g/14 oz. minced/ground turkey breast
- 35 g/½ cup fresh breadcrumbs (gluten-free if you wish)
- 1 teaspoon Thai 7 spice seasoning
- 1 teaspoon salt
- 1 teaspoon olive oil

Directions:

1. Coarsely grate the courgette/zucchini, then place in a piece of muslin/cheesecloth and squeeze out the water. Combine the grated courgette with all other ingredients except the olive oil, mixing together well. Divide the mixture into 4 equal portions and mould into burgers. Brush with oil.
2. Preheat the air-fryer to 190ºC/375ºC.
3. Add the turkey burgers to the preheated air-fryer and air-fry for 15 minutes, turning once halfway through cooking. Check the internal temperature of the burgers has reached at least 74ºC/165ºF using a meat thermometer – if not, cook for another few minutes and then serve.

Chicken And Cheese Chimichangas

Servings: 6
Cooking Time:xx
Ingredients:

- 100g shredded chicken (cooked)
- 150g nacho cheese
- 1 chopped jalapeño pepper
- 6 flour tortillas
- 5 tbsp salsa
- 60g refried beans
- 1 tsp cumin
- 0.5 tsp chill powder
- Salt and pepper to taste

Directions:

1. Take a large mixing bowl and add all of the ingredients, combining well
2. Add ⅓ of the filling to each tortilla and roll into a burrito shape
3. Spray the air fryer with cooking spray and heat to 200ºC

4. Place the chimichangas in the air fryer and cook for 7 minutes

Chicken & Potatoes

Servings: 4
Cooking Time:xx
Ingredients:

- 2 tbsp olive oil
- 2 potatoes, cut into 2" pieces
- 2 chicken breasts, cut into pieces of around 1" size
- 4 crushed garlic cloves
- 2 tsp smoked paprika
- 1 tsp thyme
- 1/2 tsp red chilli flakes
- Salt and pepper to taste

Directions:

1. Preheat your air fryer to 260ºC
2. Take a large bowl and combine the potatoes with half of the garlic, half the paprika, half the chilli flakes, salt, pepper and half the oil
3. Place into the air fryer and cook for 5 minutes, before turning over and cooking for another 5 minutes
4. Take a bowl and add the chicken with the rest of the seasonings and oil, until totally coated
5. Add the chicken to the potatoes mixture, moving the potatoes to the side
6. Cook for 10 minutes, turning the chicken halfway through

Healthy Bang Bang Chicken

Servings: 4
Cooking Time:xx
Ingredients:

- 500g chicken breasts, cut into pieces of around 1" in size
- 1 beaten egg
- 50ml milk
- 1 tbsp hot pepper sauce
- 80g flour
- 70g tapioca starch
- 1 ½ tsp seasoned starch
- 1 tsp garlic granules
- ½ tsp cumin
- 6 tbsp plain Greek yogurt
- 3 tbsp sweet chilli sauce
- 1 tsp hot sauce

Directions:

1. Preheat the air fryer to 190ºC
2. Take a mixing bowl and combine the egg, milk and hot sauce
3. Take another bowl and combine the flour, tapioca starch, salt, garlic and cumin
4. Dip the chicken pieces into the sauce bowl and then into the flour bowl
5. Place the chicken into the air fryer
6. Whilst cooking, mix together the Greek yogurt, sweet chilli sauce and hot sauce and serve with the chicken

Smoky Chicken Breast

Servings: 2
Cooking Time:xx
Ingredients:
- 2 halved chicken breasts
- 2 tsp olive oil
- 1 tsp ground thyme
- 2 tsp paprika
- 1tsp cumin
- 0.5 tsp cayenne pepper
- 0.5 tsp onion powder
- Salt and pepper to taste

Directions:
1. In a medium bowl, combine the spices together
2. Pour the spice mixture onto a plate
3. Take each chicken breast and coat in the spices, pressing down to ensure an even distribution
4. Place the chicken to one side for 5 minutes
5. Preheat your air fryer to 180ºC
6. Arrange the chicken inside the fryer and cook for 10 minutes
7. Turn the chicken over and cook for another 10 minutes
8. Remove from the fryer and allow to sit for 5 minutes before serving

Spicy Chicken Wing Drummettes

Servings: 4
Cooking Time:xx
Ingredients:
- 10 large chicken drumettes
- Cooking spray
- 100ml rice vinegar
- 3 tbsp honey
- 2 tbsp unsalted chicken stock
- 1 tbsp lower sodium soy sauce

- 1 tbsp toasted sesame oil
- ⅜ tsp crushed red pepper
- 1 garlic clove, finely chopped
- 2 tbsp chopped, unsalted, roasted peanuts
- 1 tbsp chopped fresh chives

Directions:
1. Coat the chicken in cooking spray and place inside the air fryer
2. Cook at 200ºC for 30 minutes
3. Take a mixing bowl and combine the vinegar, honey, stock, soy sauce, oil, crushed red pepper and garlic
4. Cook to a simmer, until a syrup consistency is achieved
5. Coat the chicken in this mixture and sprinkle with peanuts and chives

Satay Chicken Skewers

Servings: 4
Cooking Time:xx
Ingredients:
- 3 chicken breasts, chopped into 3 x 3-cm/1¼ x 1¼-in. cubes
- MARINADE
- 200 ml/¾ cup canned coconut milk (including the thick part from the can)
- 1 plump garlic clove, finely chopped
- 2 teaspoons freshly grated ginger
- 2 tablespoons soy sauce
- 1 heaped tablespoon peanut butter
- 1 tablespoon maple syrup
- 1 tablespoon mild curry powder
- 1 tablespoon fish sauce

Directions:
1. Mix the marinade ingredients thoroughly in a bowl, then toss in the chopped chicken and stir to coat thoroughly. Leave in the fridge to marinate for at least 4 hours.
2. Preheat the air-fryer to 190ºC/375ºF.
3. Thread the chicken onto 8 metal skewers. Add to the preheated air-fryer (you may need to cook these in two batches, depending on the size of your air-fryer). Air-fry for 10 minutes. Check the internal temperature of the chicken has reached at least 74ºC/165ºF using a meat thermometer – if not, cook for another few minutes and then serve.

Quick Chicken Nuggets

Servings: 4
Cooking Time:xx
Ingredients:

- 500g chicken tenders
- 25g ranch salad dressing mixture
- 2 tbsp plain flour
- 100g breadcrumbs
- 1 egg, beaten
- Olive oil spray

Directions:

1. Take a large mixing bowl and arrange the chicken inside
2. Sprinkle the seasoning over the top and ensure the chicken is evenly coated
3. Place the chicken to one side for around 10 minutes
4. Add the flour into a resealable bag
5. Crack the egg into a small mixing bowl and whisk
6. Pour the breadcrumbs onto a medium sized plate
7. Transfer the chicken into the resealable bag and coat with the flour, giving it a good shake
8. Remove the chicken and dip into the egg, and then rolling it into the breadcrumbs, coating evenly
9. Repeat with all pieces of the chicken
10. Heat your air fryer to 200ºC
11. Arrange the chicken inside the fryer and add a little olive oil spray to avoid sticking
12. Cook for 4 minutes, before turning over and cooking for another 4 minutes
13. Remove and serve whilst hot

Air Fryer Sesame Chicken Thighs

Servings: 4
Cooking Time:xx
Ingredients:

- 2 tbsp sesame oil
- 2 tbsp soy sauce
- 1 tbsp honey
- 1 tbsp sriracha sauce
- 1 tsp rice vinegar
- 400g chicken thighs
- 1 green onion, chopped
- 2 tbsp toasted sesame seeds

Directions:

1. Take a large bowl and combine the sesame oil, soy sauce, honey, sriracha and vinegar
2. Add the chicken and refrigerate for 30 minutes
3. Preheat the air fryer to 200ºC
4. Cook for 5 minutes
5. Flip and then cook for another 10 minutes
6. Serve with green onion and sesame seeds

Turkey And Mushroom Burgers

Servings: 2
Cooking Time:xx
Ingredients:

- 180g mushrooms
- 500g minced turkey
- 1 tbsp of your favourite chicken seasoning, e.g. Maggi
- 1 tsp onion powder
- 1 tsp garlic powder
- Salt and pepper to taste

Directions:

1. Place the mushrooms in a food processor and puree
2. Add all the seasonings and mix well
3. Remove from the food processor and transfer to a mixing bowl
4. Add the minced turkey and combine again
5. Shape the mix into 5 burger patties
6. Spray with cooking spray and place in the air fryer
7. Cook at 160ºC for 10 minutes, until cooked.

Bbq Chicken Tenders

Servings: 6
Cooking Time:xx
Ingredients:

- 300g barbecue flavoured pork rinds
- 200g all purpose flour
- 1 tbsp barbecue seasoning
- 1 egg
- 400g chicken breast tenderloins
- Cooking spray

Directions:

1. Preheat the air fryer to 190ºC
2. Place the pork rinds into a food processor and blitz to a breadcrumb consistency, before transferring to a bowl

3. In a separate bowl, combine the flour and barbecue seasoning
4. Beat the egg in a small bowl
5. Take the chicken and first dip into the egg, then the flour, and then the breadcrumbs
6. Place the chicken into the air fryer and spray with cooking spray and cook for about 15 minutes

Chicken And Wheat Stir Fry

Servings: 4
Cooking Time:xx
Ingredients:

- 1 onion
- 1 clove of garlic
- 200g skinless boneless chicken breast halves
- 3 whole tomatoes
- 400ml water
- 1 chicken stock cube
- 1 tbsp curry powder
- 130g wheat berries
- 1 tbsp vegetable oil

Directions:

1. Thinly slice the onion and garlic
2. Chop the chicken and tomatoes into cubes
3. Take a large saucepan and add the water, chicken stock, curry powder and wheat berries, combining well
4. Pour the oil into the air fryer bowl and heat for 5 minutes at 200ºC
5. Add the remaining ingredients and pour the contents into the air fryer
6. Cook for 15 minutes

Air Fryer Chicken Thigh Schnitzel

Servings: 4
Cooking Time:xx
Ingredients:

- 300g boneless chicken thighs
- 160g seasoned breadcrumbs
- 1 tsp salt
- ½ tsp ground black pepper
- 30g flour
- 1 egg
- Cooking spray

Directions:

1. Lay the chicken on a sheet of parchment paper and add another on top

2. Use a mallet or a rolling pin to flatten it down
3. Take a bowl and add the breadcrumbs with the salt and pepper
4. Place the flour into another bowl
5. Dip the chicken into the flour, then the egg, and then the breadcrumbs
6. Preheat air fryer to 190ºC
7. Place the chicken into the air fryer and spray with cooking oil
8. Cook for 6 minutes

Sticky Chicken Tikka Drumsticks

Servings: 4
Cooking Time:xx
Ingredients:

- 12 chicken drumsticks
- MARINADE
- 100 g/½ cup Greek yogurt
- 2 tablespoons tikka paste
- 2 teaspoons ginger preserve
- freshly squeezed juice of ½ a lemon
- ¾ teaspoon salt

Directions:

1. Make slices across each of the drumsticks with a sharp knife. Mix the marinade ingredients together in a bowl, then add the drumsticks. Massage the marinade into the drumsticks, then leave to marinate in the fridge overnight or for at least 6 hours.
2. Preheat the air-fryer to 200ºC/400ºF.
3. Lay the drumsticks on an air-fryer liner or a piece of pierced parchment paper. Place the paper and drumsticks in the preheated air-fryer. Air-fry for 6 minutes, then turn over and cook for a further 6 minutes. Check the internal temperature of the drumsticks has reached at least 75ºC/167ºF using a meat thermometer – if not, cook for another few minutes and then serve.

Pizza Chicken Nuggets

Servings: 2
Cooking Time:xx
Ingredients:

- 60 g/¾ cup dried breadcrumbs (see page 9)
- 20 g/¼ cup grated Parmesan
- ½ teaspoon dried oregano
- ¼ teaspoon freshly ground black pepper
- 150 g/⅔ cup Mediterranean sauce (see page 102) or 150 g/5½ oz. jarred tomato pasta sauce (keep any leftover sauce for serving)
- 400 g/14 oz. chicken fillets

Directions:

1. Preheat the air-fryer to 180°C/350°F.
2. Combine the breadcrumbs, Parmesan, oregano and pepper in a bowl. Have the Mediterranean or pasta sauce in a separate bowl.
3. Dip each chicken fillet in the tomato sauce first, then roll in the breadcrumb mix until coated fully.
4. Add the breaded fillets to the preheated air-fryer and air-fry for 10 minutes. Check the internal temperature of the chicken has reached at least 74°C/165°F using a meat thermometer – if not, cook for another few minutes.
5. Serve with some additional sauce that has been warmed through.

Keto Tandoori Chicken

Servings: 2
Cooking Time:xx
Ingredients:

- 500g chicken tenders, halved
- 1 tbsp minced ginger
- 1 tbsp minced garlic
- 1 tsp cayenne pepper
- 1 tsp turmeric
- 1 tsp garam masala
- 60ml yogurt
- 25g coriander leaves
- Salt and pepper to taste

Directions:

1. Take a large mixing bowl and combine all the ingredients, except the chicken
2. Once combined, add the chicken to the bowl and make sure it is fully coated
3. Preheat the air fryer to 160°C

4. Place the chicken in the air fryer and baste with oil
5. Cook for 10 minutes, turning over and then cooking for another 5 minutes
6. Serve whilst still warm

Chicken Fajitas

Servings: 3
Cooking Time:xx
Ingredients:

- 2 boneless chicken breasts, sliced into strips
- 5 mini (bell) peppers, sliced into strips
- 1 courgette/zucchini, sliced into 5-mm/¼-in. thick discs
- 2 tablespoons olive oil
- 28-g/1-oz. packet fajita seasoning mix
- TO SERVE
- wraps
- sliced avocado
- chopped tomato and red onion
- grated Red Leicester cheese
- plain yogurt
- coriander/cilantro
- lime wedges, for squeezing

Directions:

1. Combine the chicken, (bell) peppers, courgettes/zucchini and olive oil in a bowl. Add the fajita seasoning and stir to coat.
2. Preheat the air-fryer to 180°C/350°F.
3. Add the coated vegetables and chicken to the preheated air-fryer and air-fry for 12 minutes, shaking the drawer a couple of times during cooking. Check the internal temperature of the chicken has reached at least 74°C/165°F using a meat thermometer – if not, cook for another few minutes.
4. Serve immediately alongside the serving suggestions or your own choices of accompaniments.

Cornflake Chicken Nuggets

Servings: 4
Cooking Time:xx
Ingredients:

- 100 g/4 cups cornflakes (gluten-free if you wish)
- 70 g/½ cup plus ½ tablespoon plain/all-purpose flour (gluten-free if you wish)
- 2 eggs, beaten
- ½ teaspoon salt
- ¼ teaspoon freshly ground black pepper
- 600 g/1 lb. 5 oz. mini chicken fillets

Directions:

1. Grind the cornflakes in a food processor to a crumb-like texture. Place the flour in one bowl and the beaten eggs in a second bowl; season both bowls with the salt and pepper. Coat each chicken fillet in flour, tapping off any excess. Next dip each flour-coated chicken fillet into the egg, then the cornflakes until fully coated.
2. Preheat the air-fryer to 180ºC/350ºF.
3. Add the chicken fillets to the preheated air-fryer (you may need to add the fillets in two batches, depending on the size of your air-fryer) and air-fry for 10 minutes, turning halfway through cooking. Check the internal temperature of the nuggets has reached at least 74ºC/165ºF using a meat thermometer – if not, cook for another few minutes and then serve.
4. VARIATION: SIMPLE CHICKEN NUGGETS
5. For a simpler version, replace the crushed cornflakes with 90 g/1¼ cups dried breadcrumbs (see page 9). Prepare and air-fry in the same way.

Chicken Parmesan With Marinara Sauce

Servings: 4
Cooking Time:xx
Ingredients:

- 400g chicken breasts, sliced in half
- 250g panko breadcrumbs
- 140g grated parmesan cheese
- 140g grated mozzarella cheese
- 3 egg whites
- 200g marinara sauce
- 2 tsp Italian seasoning
- Salt and pepper to taste
- Cooking spray

Directions:

1. Preheat the air fryer to 200ºC
2. Lay the chicken slices on the work surface and pound with a mallet or a rolling pin to flatten
3. Take a mixing bowl and add the panko breadcrumbs, cheese and the seasoning, combining well
4. Add the egg whites into a separate bowl
5. Dip the chicken into the egg whites and then the breadcrumbs
6. Cook for 7 minutes in the air fryer

Chicken Tikka Masala

Servings: 4
Cooking Time:xx
Ingredients:

- 100g tikka masala curry pasta
- 200g low fat yogurt
- 600g skinless chicken breasts
- 1 tbsp vegetable oil
- 1 onion, chopped
- 400g can of the whole, peeled tomatoes
- 20ml water
- 1 tbsp sugar
- 2 tbsp lemon juice
- 1 small bunch of chopped coriander leaves

Directions:

1. Take a bowl and combine the tikka masala curry paste with half the yogurt
2. Cut the chicken into strips
3. Preheat the air fryer to 200ºC
4. Add the yogurt mixture and coat the chicken until fully covered
5. Place into the refrigerator for 2 hours
6. Place the oil and onion in the air fryer and cook for 10 minutes
7. Add the marinated chicken, tomatoes, water and the rest of the yogurt and combine
8. Add the sugar and lemon juice and combine again
9. Cook for 15 minutes

Charred Chicken Breasts

Servings: 2
Cooking Time:xx
Ingredients:

- 2 tsp paprika
- 1 tsp ground thyme
- 1 tsp cumin
- ½ tsp cayenne pepper
- ½ tsp onion powder
- ½ tsp black pepper
- ¼ tsp salt
- 2 tsp vegetable oil
- 2 skinless boneless chicken breasts, cut into halves

Directions:

1. Take a bowl and add the paprika, thyme, cumin, cayenne pepper, onion powder, black pepper and salt
2. Coat each chicken breast with oil and dredge chicken in the spice mixture
3. Preheat air fryer to 175C
4. Cook for 10 minutes and flip
5. Cook for 10 more minutes

Nashville Chicken

Servings: 4
Cooking Time:xx
Ingredients:

- 400g boneless chicken breast tenders
- 2 tsp salt
- 2 tsp coarsely ground black pepper
- 2 tbsp hot sauce
- 2 tbsp pickle juice
- 500g all purpose flour
- 3 large eggs
- 300ml buttermilk
- 2 tbsp olive oil
- 6 tbsp cayenne pepper
- 3 tbsp dark brown sugar
- 1 tsp chilli powder
- 1 tsp garlic powder
- 1 tsp paprika
- Salt and pepper to taste

Directions:

1. Take a large mixing bowl and add the chicken, hot sauce, pickle juice, salt and pepper and combine
2. Place in the refrigerator for 3 hours
3. Transfer the flour to a bowl
4. Take another bowl and add the eggs, buttermilk and 1 tbsp of the hot sauce, combining well
5. Press each piece of chicken into the flour and coat well
6. Place the chicken into the buttermilk mixture and then back into the flour
7. Allow to sit or 10 minutes
8. Preheat the air fryer to 193C
9. Whisk together the spices, brown sugar and olive oil to make the sauce and pour over the chicken tenders
10. Serve whilst still warm

Bacon Wrapped Chicken Thighs

Servings: 4
Cooking Time:xx
Ingredients:

- 75g softened butter
- ½ clove minced garlic
- ¼ tsp dried thyme
- ¼ tsp dried basil
- ⅛ tsp coarse salt
- 100g thick cut bacon
- 350g chicken thighs, boneless and skinless
- 2 tsp minced garlic
- Salt and pepper to taste

Directions:

1. Take a mixing bowl and add the softened butter, garlic, thyme, basil, salt and pepper, combining well
2. Place the butter onto a sheet of plastic wrap and roll up to make a butter log
3. Refrigerate for about 2 hours
4. Remove the plastic wrap
5. Place one bacon strip onto the butter and then place the chicken thighs on top of the bacon. Sprinkle with garlic
6. Place the cold butter into the middle of the chicken thigh and tuck one end of bacon into the chicken
7. Next, fold over the chicken thigh whilst rolling the bacon around
8. Repeat with the rest
9. Preheat the air fryer to 188C
10. Cook the chicken until white in the centre and the juices run clear

Crunchy Chicken Tenders

Servings: 4
Cooking Time:xx

Ingredients:

- 8 regular chicken tenders (frozen work best)
- 1 egg
- 2 tbsp olive oil
- 150g dried breadcrumbs

Directions:

1. Heat the fryer to 175ºC
2. In a small bowl, beat the egg
3. In another bowl, combine the oil and the breadcrumbs together
4. Take one tender and first dip it into the egg, and then cover it in the breadcrumb mixture
5. Place the tender into the fryer basket
6. Repeat with the rest of the tenders, arranging them carefully so they don't touch inside the basket
7. Cook for 12 minutes, checking that they are white in the centre before serving

Honey Cajun Chicken Thighs

Servings: 6
Cooking Time:xx

Ingredients:

- 100ml buttermilk
- 1 tsp hot sauce
- 400g skinless, boneless chicken thighs
- 150g all purpose flour
- 60g tapioca flour
- 2.5 tsp cajun seasoning
- ½ tsp garlic salt
- ½ tsp honey powder
- ¼ tsp ground paprika
- ⅛ tsp cayenne pepper
- 4 tsp honey

Directions:

1. Take a large bowl and combine the buttermilk and hot sauce
2. Transfer to a plastic bag and add the chicken thighs
3. Allow to marinate for 30 minutes
4. Take another bowl and add the flour, tapioca flour, cajun seasoning, garlic, salt, honey powder, paprika, and cayenne pepper, combining well
5. Dredge the chicken through the mixture
6. Preheat the air fryer to 175C

7. Cook for 15 minutes before flipping the thighs over and cooking for another 10 minutes
8. Drizzle 1 tsp of honey over each thigh

Grain-free Chicken Katsu

Servings: 4
Cooking Time:xx

Ingredients:

- 125 g/1¼ cups ground almonds
- ½ teaspoon salt
- ½ teaspoon garlic powder
- ½ teaspoon dried parsley
- ½ teaspoon freshly ground black pepper
- ¼ teaspoon onion powder
- ¼ teaspoon dried oregano
- 450 g/1 lb. mini chicken fillets
- 1 egg, beaten
- oil, for spraying/drizzling
- coriander/cilantro leaves, to serve
- KATSU SAUCE
- 1 teaspoon olive oil or avocado oil
- 1 courgette/zucchini (approx. 150 g/5 oz.), finely chopped
- 1 carrot (approx. 100 g/3½ oz.), finely chopped
- 1 onion (approx. 120 g/4½ oz.), finely chopped
- 1 eating apple (approx. 150 g/5 oz.), cored and finely chopped
- 1 teaspoon ground ginger
- 1 teaspoon ground turmeric
- 2 teaspoons ground cumin
- 2 teaspoons ground coriander
- 1½ teaspoons mild chilli/chili powder
- 1 teaspoon garlic powder
- 1½ tablespoons runny honey
- 1 tablespoon soy sauce (gluten-free if you wish)
- 700 ml/3 cups vegetable stock (700 ml/3 cups water with 1½ stock cubes)

Directions:

1. First make the sauce. The easiest way to ensure all the vegetables and apple are finely chopped is to combine them in a food processor. Heat the oil in a large saucepan and sauté the finely chopped vegetables and apple for 5 minutes. Add all the seasonings, honey, soy sauce and stock and stir well, then bring to a simmer and simmer for 30 minutes.
2. Meanwhile, mix together the ground almonds, seasonings and spices. Dip each chicken fillet

into the beaten egg, then into the almond-spice mix, making sure each fillet is fully coated. Spray the coated chicken fillets with olive oil (or simply drizzle over).

3. Preheat the air-fryer to 180ºC/350ºF.

4. Place the chicken fillets in the preheated air-fryer and air-fry for 10 minutes, turning halfway through cooking. Check the internal temperature of the chicken has reached at least 74ºC/165ºF using a meat thermometer – if not, cook for another few minutes.

5. Blend the cooked sauce in a food processor until smooth. Serve the chicken with the Katsu Sauce drizzled over (if necessary, reheat the sauce gently before serving) and scattered with coriander leaves. Any unused sauce can be frozen.

Chicken Fried Rice

Servings: 4
Cooking Time:xx
Ingredients:

- 400g cooked white rice
- 400g cooked chicken, diced
- 200g frozen peas and carrots
- 6 tbsp soy sauce
- 1 tbsp vegetable oil
- 1 diced onion

Directions:

1. Take a large bowl and add the rice, vegetable oil and soy sauce and combine well

2. Add the frozen peas, carrots, diced onion and the chicken and mix together well

3. Pour the mixture into a nonstick pan

4. Place the pan into the air fryer

5. Cook at 182C for 20 minutes

Chicken Kiev

Servings: 4
Cooking Time:xx
Ingredients:

- 4 boneless chicken breasts
- 4 tablespoons plain/all-purpose flour (gluten-free if you wish)
- 1 egg, beaten
- 130 g/2 cups dried breadcrumbs (gluten-free if you wish, see page 9)
- GARLIC BUTTER
- 60 g/4 tablespoons salted butter, softened
- 1 large garlic clove, finely chopped

Directions:

1. Mash together the butter and garlic. Form into a sausage shape, then slice into 4 equal discs. Place in the freezer until frozen.

2. Make a deep horizontal slit across each chicken breast, taking care not to cut through to the other side. Stuff the cavity with a disc of frozen garlic butter. Place the flour in a shallow bowl, the egg in another and the breadcrumbs in a third. Coat each chicken breast first in flour, then egg, then breadcrumbs.

3. Preheat the air-fryer to 180ºC/350ºF.

4. Add the chicken Kievs to the preheated air-fryer and air-fry for 12 minutes until cooked through. This is hard to gauge as the butter inside the breast is not an indicator of doneness, so test the meat in the centre with a meat thermometer – it should be at least 75ºC/167ºF; if not, cook for another few minutes.

Crispy Cornish Hen

Servings: 4
Cooking Time:xx
Ingredients:

- 2 Cornish hens, weighing around 500g each
- 2 tbsp olive oil
- 1 tsp garlic powder
- 1 tsp paprika
- 1.5 tsp Italian seasoning
- 1 tbsp lemon juice
- Salt and pepper to taste

Directions:

1. Preheat your air fryer to 260ºC

2. Combine all the ingredients into a bowl (except for the hens) until smooth

3. Brush the hens with the mixture, coating evenly

4. Place in the air fryer basket, with the breast side facing down

5. Cook for 35 minutes

6. Turn over and cook for another 10 minutes

7. Ensure the hens are white in the middle before serving

Air Fryer Bbq Chicken

Servings: 4
Cooking Time:xx
Ingredients:

- 1 whole chicken
- 2 tbsp avocado oil
- 1 tbsp kosher salt
- 1 tsp ground pepper
- 1 tsp garlic powder
- 1 tsp paprika
- ½ tsp dried basil
- ½ tsp dried oregano
- ½ tsp dried thyme

Directions:

1. Mix the seasonings together and spread over chicken
2. Place the chicken in the air fryer breast side down
3. Cook at 182C for 50 minutes and then breast side up for 10 minutes
4. Carve and serve

Garlic Parmesan Fried Chicken Wings

Servings: 4
Cooking Time:xx
Ingredients:

- 16 chicken wing drumettes
- Cooking spray
- 240ml low fat buttermilk
- 150g flour
- 140g grated parmesan
- 2 tbsp low sodium soy sauce
- 1 sachet of your favourite chicken seasoning
- 1 tsp garlic powder
- Salt and pepper to taste

Directions:

1. Place the chicken onto a cooking tray and pour the soy sauce over the top, ensuring it is fully coated
2. Season the chicken and place in the refrigerator for 30 minutes
3. Add the flour and parmesan into a ziplock bag
4. Coat the chicken with buttermilk and add it to the ziplock bag with the flour
5. Preheat your air fryer to 200ºC
6. Place the chicken into the air fryer for 20 minutes

7. Shake the air fryer basket every 5 minutes until the 20 minutes is up

Air Fried Maple Chicken Thighs

Servings: 4
Cooking Time:xx
Ingredients:

- 200ml buttermilk
- ½ tbsp maple syrup
- 1 egg
- 1 tsp granulated garlic salt
- 4 chicken thighs with the bone in
- 140g all purpose flour
- 65g tapioca flour
- 1 tsp sweet paprika
- 1 tsp onion powder
- ¼ tsp ground black pepper
- ¼ tsp cayenne pepper
- ½ tsp granulated garlic
- ½ tsp honey powder

Directions:

1. Take a bowl and combine the buttermilk, maple syrup, egg and garlic powder
2. Transfer to a bag and add chicken thighs, shaking to combine well
3. Set aside for 1 hour
4. Take a shallow bowl and add the flour, tapioca flour, salt, sweet paprika, smoked paprika, pepper, cayenne pepper and honey powder, combining well
5. Preheat the air fryer to 190ºC
6. Drag the chicken through flour mixture and place the chicken skin side down in the air fryer Cook for 12 minutes, until white in the middle

Orange Chicken

Servings: 2
Cooking Time:xx
Ingredients:

- 600g chicken thighs, boneless and skinless
- 2 tbsp cornstarch
- 60ml orange juice
- 1 tbsp soy sauce
- 2 tbsp brown sugar
- 1 tbsp rice wine vinegar
- 1/4 teaspoon ground ginger
- Pinch of red pepper flakes

- Zest of one orange
- 2 tsp water and 2 tsp cornstarch mixed together

Directions:
1. Preheat your air fryer to 250°C
2. Take a bowl and combine the chicken with the cornstarch
3. Place in the air fryer and cook for 9 minutes
4. Take a bowl and combine the rest of the ingredients, except for the water and cornstarch mixture
5. Place in a saucepan and bring to the boil and then turn down to a simmer for 5 minutes
6. Add the water and cornstarch mixture to the pan and combine well
7. Remove the chicken from the fryer and pour the sauce over the top

Chicken Balls, Greek-style

Servings: 4
Cooking Time:xx
Ingredients:
- 500g ground chicken
- 1 egg
- 1 tbsp dried oregano
- 1.5 tbsp garlic paste
- 1 tsp lemon zest
- 1 tsp dried onion powder
- Salt and pepper to taste

Directions:
1. Take a bowl and combine all ingredients well
2. Use your hands to create meatballs - you should be able to make 12 balls
3. Preheat your air fryer to 260°C
4. Add the meatballs to the fryer and cook for 9 minutes

Hawaiian Chicken

Servings: 2
Cooking Time:xx
Ingredients:
- 2 chicken breasts
- 1 tbsp butter
- A pinch of salt and pepper
- 160ml pineapple juice
- 25g brown sugar
- 3 tbsp soy sauce
- 2 tsp water
- 1 clove of garlic, minced
- 1 tsp grated ginger

- 2 tsp cornstarch

Directions:
1. Preheat the air fryer to 260°C
2. Take a bowl and combine the butter and salt and pepper
3. Cover the chicken with the butter and cook in the fryer for 15 minutes, turning halfway
4. Remove and allow to rest for 5 minutes
5. Take another bowl and mix together the pineapple juice, soy sauce, garlic, ginger, and brown sugar
6. Transfer to a saucepan and simmer for 5 minutes
7. Combine the water and cornstarch and add to the sauce, stirring continually for another minute
8. Slice the chicken into strips and pour the sauce over the top

Pepper & Lemon Chicken Wings

Servings: 2
Cooking Time:xx
Ingredients:
- 1kg chicken wings
- 1/4 tsp cayenne pepper
- 2 tsp lemon pepper seasoning
- 3 tbsp butter
- 1 tsp honey
- An extra 1 tsp lemon pepper seasoning for the sauce

Directions:
1. Preheat the air fryer to 260°C
2. Place the lemon pepper seasoning and cayenne in a bowl and combine
3. Coat the chicken in the seasoning
4. Place the chicken in the air fryer and cook for 20 minutes, turning over halfway
5. Turn the temperature up to 300°C and cook for another 6 minutes
6. Meanwhile, melt the butter and combine with the honey and the rest of the seasoning
7. Remove the wings from the air fryer and pour the sauce over the top

Olive Stained Turkey Breast

Servings: 14
Cooking Time:xx
Ingredients:

- The brine from a can of olives
- 150ml buttermilk
- 300g boneless and skinless turkey breasts
- 1 sprig fresh rosemary
- 2 sprigs fresh thyme

Directions:

1. Take a mixing bowl and combine the olive brine and buttermilk
2. Pour the mixture over the turkey breast
3. Add the rosemary and thyme sprigs
4. Place into the refrigerator for 8 hours
5. Remove from the fridge and let the turkey reach room temperature
6. Preheat the air fryer to 175C
7. Cook for 15 minutes, ensuring the turkey is cooked through before serving

Chicken Tikka

Servings: 2
Cooking Time:xx
Ingredients:

- 2 chicken breasts, diced
- FIRST MARINADE
- freshly squeezed juice of ½ a lemon
- 1 tablespoon freshly grated ginger
- 1 tablespoon freshly grated garlic
- a good pinch of salt
- SECOND MARINADE
- 100 g/½ cup Greek yogurt
- ½ teaspoon chilli powder
- ½ teaspoon chilli paste
- ½ teaspoon turmeric
- ½ teaspoon garam masala
- 1 tablespoon olive oil

Directions:

1. Mix the ingredients for the first marinade together in a bowl, add in the chicken and stir to coat all the chicken pieces. Leave in the fridge to marinate for 20 minutes.
2. Combine the second marinade ingredients. Once the first marinade has had 20 minutes, add the second marinade to the chicken and stir well. Leave in the fridge for at least 4 hours.
3. Preheat the air-fryer to 180°C/350°F.

4. Thread the chicken pieces onto metal skewers that fit in your air-fryer. Add the skewers to the preheated air-fryer and air-fry for 10 minutes. Check the internal temperature of the chicken has reached at least 74°C/165°F using a meat thermometer – if not, cook for another few minutes and then serve.

Whole Chicken

Servings: 4
Cooking Time:xx
Ingredients:

- 1.5-kg/3¼-lb. chicken
- 2 tablespoons butter or coconut oil
- salt and freshly ground black pepper

Directions:

1. Place the chicken breast-side up and carefully insert the butter or oil between the skin and the flesh of each breast. Season.
2. Preheat the air-fryer to 180°C/350°F. If the chicken hits the heating element, remove the drawer to lower the chicken a level.
3. Add the chicken to the preheated air-fryer breast-side up. Air-fry for 30 minutes, then turn over and cook for a further 10 minutes. Check the internal temperature with a meat thermometer. If it is 75°C/167°F at the thickest part, remove the chicken from the air-fryer and leave to rest for 10 minutes before carving. If less than 75°C/167°F, continue to cook until this internal temperature is reached and then allow to rest.

Chicken Jalfrezi

Servings: 4
Cooking Time:xx
Ingredients:

- 500g chicken breasts
- 1 tbsp water
- 4 tbsp tomato sauce
- 1 chopped onion
- 1 chopped bell pepper
- 2 tsp love oil
- 1 tsp turmeric
- 1 tsp cayenne pepper
- 2 tsp garam masala
- Salt and pepper to taste

Directions:

1. Take a large mixing bowl and add the chicken, onions, pepper, salt, garam masala, turmeric, oil and cayenne pepper, combining well
2. Place the chicken mix in the air fryer and cook at 180°C for 15 minutes
3. Take a microwave-safe bowl and add the tomato sauce, water salt, garam masala and cayenne, combining well
4. Cook in the microwave for 1 minute, stir then cook for a further minute
5. Remove the chicken from the air fryer and pour the sauce over the top.
6. Serve whilst still warm

Buffalo Wings

Servings: 4
Cooking Time:xx
Ingredients:
- 500g chicken wings
- 1 tbsp olive oil
- 5 tbsp cayenne pepper sauce
- 75g butter
- 2 tbsp vinegar
- 1 tsp garlic powder
- ¼ tsp cayenne pepper

Directions:
1. Preheat the air fryer to 182C
2. Take a large mixing bowl and add the chicken wings
3. Drizzle oil over the wings, coating evenly
4. Cook for 25 minutes and then flip the wings and cook for 5 more minutes
5. In a saucepan over a medium heat, mix the hot pepper sauce, butter, vinegar, garlic powder and cayenne pepper, combining well
6. Pour the sauce over the wings and flip to coat, before serving

Chicken Milanese

Servings: 4
Cooking Time:xx
Ingredients:
- 130 g/1¾ cups dried breadcrumbs (gluten-free if you wish, see page 9)
- 50 g/⅔ cup grated Parmesan
- 1 teaspoon dried basil
- ½ teaspoon dried thyme
- ¼ teaspoon freshly ground black pepper
- 1 egg, beaten

- 4 tablespoons plain/all-purpose flour (gluten-free if you wish)
- 4 boneless chicken breasts

Directions:
1. Combine the breadcrumbs, cheese, herbs and pepper in a bowl. In a second bowl beat the egg, and in the third bowl have the plain/all-purpose flour. Dip each chicken breast first into the flour, then the egg, then the seasoned breadcrumbs.
2. Preheat the air-fryer to 180°C/350°F.
3. Add the breaded chicken breasts to the preheated air-fryer and air-fry for 12 minutes. Check the internal temperature of the chicken has reached at least 74°C/165°F using a meat thermometer – if not, cook for another few minutes.

Buffalo Chicken Wontons

Servings: 6
Cooking Time:xx
Ingredients:
- 200g shredded chicken
- 1 tbsp buffalo sauce
- 4 tbsp softened cream cheese
- 1 sliced spring onion
- 2 tbsp blue cheese crumbles
- 12 wonton wrappers

Directions:
1. Preheat the air fryer to 200°C
2. Take a bowl and combine the chicken and buffalo sauce
3. In another bowl mix the cream cheese until a smooth consistency has formed and then combine the scallion blue cheese and seasoned chicken
4. Take the wonton wrappers and run wet fingers along each edge
5. Place 1 tbsp of the filling into the centre of the wonton and fold the corners together
6. Cook at 200°C for 3 to 5 minutes, until golden brown

Buttermilk Chicken

Servings: 4
Cooking Time:xx

Ingredients:

- 500g chicken thighs, skinless and boneless
- 180ml buttermilk
- 40g tapioca flour
- ½ tsp garlic salt
- 1 egg
- 75g all purpose flour
- ½ tsp brown sugar
- 1 tsp garlic powder
- ½ tsp paprika
- ½ tsp onion powder
- ¼ tsp oregano
- Salt and pepper to taste

Directions:

1. Take a medium mixing bowl and combine the buttermilk and hot sauce
2. Add the tapioca flour, garlic salt and black pepper in a plastic bag and shake
3. Beat the egg
4. Take the chicken thighs and tip into the buttermilk, then the tapioca mixture, the egg, and then the flour
5. Preheat air fryer to 190°C
6. Cook the chicken thighs for 10 minutes, until white in the middle

Cheddar & Bbq Stuffed Chicken

Servings: 2
Cooking Time:xx

Ingredients:

- 3 strips of bacon
- 100g cheddar cheese
- 3 tbsp barbecue sauce
- 300g skinless and boneless chicken breasts
- salt and ground pepper to taste

Directions:

1. Preheat the air fryer to 190°C
2. Cook one of the back strips for 2 minutes, before cutting into small pieces
3. Increase the temperature of the air fryer to 200°C
4. Mix together the cooked bacon, cheddar cheese and 1 tbsp barbecue sauce
5. Take the chicken and make a pouch by cutting a 1 inch gap into the top
6. Stuff the pouch with the bacon and cheese mixture and then wrap around the chicken breast
7. Coat the chicken with the rest of the BBQ sauce
8. Cook for 10 minutes in the air fryer, before turning and cooking for an additional 10 minutes

Sauces & Snack And Appetiser Recipes

Garlic Cheese Bread

Servings: 2
Cooking Time:xx
Ingredients:

- 250g grated mozzarella
- 50g grated parmesan
- 1 egg
- ½ tsp garlic powder

Directions:

1. Line air fryer with parchment paper
2. Mix ingredients in a bowl
3. Press into a circle onto the parchment paper in the air fryer
4. Heat the air fryer to 175°C
5. Cook for 10 minutes

Spicy Egg Rolls

Servings: 4
Cooking Time:xx
Ingredients:

- 1 rotisserie chicken, shredded and diced
- 3 tbsp water
- 3 tbsp taco seasoning
- 1 can of black beans, drained
- 1 red bell pepper, diced
- 1 can of sweetcorn, drained
- 1 jalapeño pepper, deseeded and minced
- 2 packs of egg roll wrappers
- 250g grated strong cheddar cheese
- 250g grated Monterey Jack cheese

Directions:

1. Take a medium bowl and add the water and taco seasoning, combining well
2. Add the shredded check and coat well
3. Lay out an egg roll wrapper and arrange it so that one corner is facing towards you
4. Add 3 tablespoons of the mixture into the wrapper, just below the middle
5. Roll the corner facing you upwards, pulling it tightly closed over the mixture
6. Add a little water to the other two corners and fold into the centre and pat down to seal
7. Roll the rest of the wrapper up, so that all the corners are sealed
8. Repeat with the rest of the mixture

9. Preheat the air fryer to 220°C
10. Cook for 9 minutes and turn over at the halfway point

Mini Calzones

Servings: 16
Cooking Time:xx
Ingredients:

- Flour for rolling out the dough
- 1 round pizza dough
- 100g pizza sauce

Directions:

1. Roll out the dough to ¼ inch thick
2. Cut out 8-10 dough rounds using a cutter
3. Re-roll the dough and cut out another 6 rounds
4. Top each round with pizza sauce, cheese and pepperoni
5. Fold dough over and pinch the edges to seal
6. Heat the air fryer to 190°C
7. Place the calzone in the air fryer and cook for about 8 minutes until golden brown

Potato Patties

Servings: 12
Cooking Time:xx
Ingredients:

- 150g instant mash
- 50g peas and carrots
- 2 tbsp coriander
- 1 tbsp oil
- 100ml hot water
- ½ tsp turmeric
- ½ tsp cayenne
- ½ tsp salt
- ½ tsp cumin seeds
- ¼ tsp ground cumin

Directions:

1. Place all the ingredients in a bowl. Mix well cover and stand for 10 minutes
2. Preheat the air fryer to 200°C
3. Spray the air fryer with cooking spray
4. Make 12 patties, place in the air fryer and cook for 10 minutes

Mac & Cheese Bites

Servings: 14
Cooking Time:xx
Ingredients:

- 200g mac and cheese
- 2 eggs
- 200g panko breadcrumbs
- Cooking spray

Directions:

1. Place drops of mac and cheese on parchment paper and freeze for 1 hour
2. Beat the eggs in a bowl, add the breadcrumbs to another bowl
3. Dip the mac and cheese balls in the egg then into the breadcrumbs
4. Heat the air fryer to 190°C
5. Place in the air fryer, spray with cooking spray and cook for 15 minutes

Scotch Eggs

Servings: 6
Cooking Time:xx
Ingredients:

- 300g pork sausage
- 6 hard boiled eggs, shelled
- 50g cup flour
- 2 eggs, beaten
- 1 cup breadcrumbs
- Cooking spray

Directions:

1. Divide sausage into 6 portions
2. Place an egg in the middle of each portion and wrap around the egg
3. Dip the sausage in flour, then egg and then coat in breadcrumbs
4. Place in the air fryer and cook at 200°C for 12 minutes

Tasty Pumpkin Seeds

Servings: 2
Cooking Time:xx
Ingredients:

- 1 ¾ cups pumpkin seeds
- 2 tsp avocado oil
- 1 tsp paprika
- 1 tsp salt

Directions:

1. Preheat air fryer to 180°C
2. Add all ingredients to a bowl and mix well

3. Place in the air fryer and cook for 35 minutes shaking frequently

Jalapeño Pockets

Servings: 4
Cooking Time:xx
Ingredients:

- 1 chopped onion
- 60g cream cheese
- 1 jalapeño, chopped
- 8 wonton wrappers
- ¼ tsp garlic powder
- ⅛ tsp onion powder

Directions:

1. Cook the onion in a pan for 5 minutes until softened
2. Add to a bowl and mix with the remaining ingredients
3. Lay the wonton wrappers out and add filling to each one
4. Fold over to create a triangle and seal with water around the edges
5. Heat the air fryer to 200°C
6. Place in the air fryer and cook for about 4 minutes

Spicy Peanuts

Servings: 8
Cooking Time:xx
Ingredients:

- 2 tbsp olive oil
- 3 tbsp seafood seasoning
- ½ tsp cayenne
- 300g raw peanuts
- Salt to taste

Directions:

1. Preheat the air fryer to 160°C
2. Whisk together ingredients in a bowl and stir in the peanuts
3. Add to air fryer and cook for 10 minutes, shake then cook for a further 10 minutes
4. Sprinkle with salt and cook for another 5 minutes

Tortellini Bites

Servings: 6
Cooking Time:xx
Ingredients:

- 200g cheese tortellini
- 150g flour
- 100g panko bread crumbs
- 50g grated parmesan
- 1 tsp dried oregano
- 2 eggs
- ½ tsp garlic powder
- ½ tsp chilli flakes
- Salt
- Pepper

Directions:

1. Cook the tortellini according to the packet instructions
2. Mix the panko, parmesan, oregano, garlic powder, chilli flakes salt and pepper in a bowl
3. Beat the eggs in another bowl and place the flour in a third bowl
4. Coat the tortellini in flour, then egg and then in the panko mix
5. Place in the air fryer and cook at 185°C for 10 minutes until crispy
6. Serve with marinara sauce for dipping

Cheesy Taco Crescents

Servings: 8
Cooking Time:xx
Ingredients:

- 1 can Pillsbury crescent sheets, or alternative
- 4 Monterey Jack cheese sticks
- 150g browned minced beef
- ½ pack taco seasoning mix

Directions:

1. Preheat the air fryer to 200°C
2. Combine the minced beef and the taco seasoning, warm in the microwave for about 2 minutes
3. Cut the crescent sheets into 8 equal squares
4. Cut the cheese sticks in half
5. Add half a cheese stick to each square, and 2 tablespoons of mince
6. Roll up the dough and pinch at the ends to seal
7. Place in the air fryer and cook for 5 minutes
8. Turnover and cook for another 3 minutes

Snack Style Falafel

Servings: 15
Cooking Time:xx
Ingredients:

- 150g dry garbanzo beans
- 300g coriander
- 75g flat leaf parsley
- 1 red onion, quartered
- 1 clove garlic
- 2 tbsp chickpea flour
- Cooking spray
- 1 tbsp cumin
- 1 tbsp coriander
- 1 tbsp sriracha
- ½ tsp baking powder
- Salt and pepper to taste
- ¼ tsp baking soda

Directions:

1. Add all ingredients apart from the baking soda and baking powder to a food processor and blend well
2. Cover and rest for 1 hour
3. Heat air fryer to 190°C
4. Add baking powder and baking soda to mix and combine
5. Form mix into 15 equal balls
6. Spray air fryer with cooking spray
7. Add to air fryer and cook for 8-10 minutes

Roasted Almonds

Servings: 2
Cooking Time:xx
Ingredients:

- 1 tbsp soy sauce
- 1 tbsp garlic powder
- 1 tsp paprika
- ¼ tsp pepper
- 400g raw almonds

Directions:

1. Place all of the ingredients apart from the almonds in a bowl and mix
2. Add the almonds and coat well
3. Place the almonds in the air fryer and cook at 160°C for 6 minutes shaking every 2 minutes

Mini Aubergine Parmesan Pizza

Servings: 8
Cooking Time:xx
Ingredients:

- 1 aubergine, cut into ½ inch slices
- Salt to taste
- 1 egg
- 1 tbsp water
- 100g bread crumbs
- 75g grated parmesan
- 6 tbsp pizza sauce
- 50g sliced olives
- 75g grated mozzarella
- Basil to garnish

Directions:

1. Preheat air fryer to 160ºC
2. Mix egg and water together and in another bowl mix the breadcrumbs and parmesan
3. Dip the aubergine in the egg then coat with the breadcrumbs
4. Place in the air fryer and cook for 10 minutes
5. Spoon pizza sauce on the aubergine, add olives and sprinkle with mozzarella
6. Cook for about 4 minutes until cheese has melted

Waffle Fries

Servings: 4
Cooking Time:xx
Ingredients:

- 2 large potatoes, russet potatoes work best
- 1 tsp salt for seasoning
- Waffle cutter

Directions:

1. Peel the potatoes and slice using the waffle cutter. You can also use a mandolin cutter that has a blade
2. Transfer the potatoes to a bowl and season with the salt, coating evenly
3. Add to the air fryer and cook at 220ºC for 15 minutes, shaking every so often

Pasta Chips

Servings: 2
Cooking Time:xx
Ingredients:

- 300g dry pasta bows
- 1 tbsp olive oil
- 1 tbsp nutritional yeast
- 1½ tsp Italian seasoning
- ½ tsp salt

Directions:

1. Cook the pasta for half the time stated on the packet
2. Drain and mix with the oil, yeast, seasoning and salt
3. Place in the air fryer and cook at 200ºC for 5 minutes shake and cook for a further 3 minutes until crunchy

Pork Jerky

Servings: 35
Cooking Time:xx
Ingredients:

- 300g mince pork
- 1 tbsp oil
- 1 tbsp sriracha
- 1 tbsp soy
- ½ tsp pink curing salt
- 1 tbsp rice vinegar
- ½ tsp salt
- ½ tsp pepper
- ½ tsp onion powder

Directions:

1. Mix all ingredients in a bowl until combined
2. Refrigerate for about 8 hours
3. Shape into sticks and place in the air fryer
4. Heat the air fryer to 160ºC
5. Cook for 1 hour turn then cook for another hour
6. Turn again and cook for another hour
7. Cover with paper and sit for 8 hours

Pretzel Bites

Servings: 2
Cooking Time:xx
Ingredients:

- 650g flour
- 2.5 tsp active dry yeast
- 260ml hot water
- 1 tsp salt
- 4 tbsp melted butter
- 2 tbsp sugar

Directions:

1. Take a large bowl and add the flour, sugar and salt

2. Take another bowl and combine the hot water and yeast, stirring until the yeast has dissolved
3. Then, add the yeast mixture to the flour mixture and use your hands to combine
4. Knead for 2 minutes
5. Cover the bowl with a kitchen towel for around half an hour
6. Divide the dough into 6 pieces
7. Preheat the air fryer to 260°C
8. Take each section of dough and tear off a piece, rolling it in your hands to create a rope shape, that is around 1" in thickness
9. Cut into 2" strips
10. Place the small dough balls into the air fryer and leave a little space in-between
11. Cook for 6 minutes
12. Once cooked, remove and brush with melted butter and sprinkle salt on top

Salt And Vinegar Chips

Servings: 4
Cooking Time:xx
Ingredients:

- 6-10 Jerusalem artichokes, thinly sliced
- 150ml apple cider vinegar
- 2 tbsp olive oil
- Sea salt

Directions:

1. Soak the artichoke in apple cider vinegar for 20-30 minutes
2. Preheat the air fryer to 200°C
3. Coat the artichoke in olive oil
4. Place in the air fryer and cook for 15 Minutes
5. Sprinkle with salt

Spring Rolls

Servings: 20
Cooking Time:xx
Ingredients:

- 160g dried rice noodles
- 1 tsp sesame oil
- 300g minced beef
- 200g frozen vegetables
- 1 onion, diced
- 3 cloves garlic, crushed
- 1 tsp soy sauce
- 1 tbsp vegetable oil
- 1 pack egg roll wrappers

Directions:

1. Soak the noodles in a bowl of water until soft
2. Add the minced beef, onion, garlic and vegetables to a pan and cook for 6 minutes
3. Remove from the heat, stir in the noodles and add the soy
4. Heat the air fryer to 175°C
5. Add a diagonal strip of filling in each egg roll wrapper
6. Fold the top corner over the filling, fold in the two side corners
7. Brush the centre with water and roll to seal
8. Brush with vegetable oil, place in the air fryer and cook for about 8 minutes until browned

Salt And Vinegar Chickpeas

Servings: 5
Cooking Time:xx
Ingredients:

- 1 can chickpeas
- 100ml white vinegar
- 1 tbsp olive oil
- Salt to taste

Directions:

1. Combine chickpeas and vinegar in a pan, simmer remove from heat and stand for 30 minutes
2. Preheat the air fryer to 190°C
3. Drain chickpeas
4. Place chickpeas in the air fryer and cook for about 4 minutes
5. Pour chickpeas into an ovenproof bowl drizzle with oil, sprinkle with salt
6. Place bowl in the air fryer and cook for another 4 minutes

Asian Devilled Eggs

Servings: 12
Cooking Time:xx
Ingredients:

- 6 large eggs
- 2 tbsp mayo
- 1 ½ tsp sriracha
- 1 ½ tsp sesame oil
- 1 tsp soy sauce
- 1 tsp dijon mustard
- 1 tsp finely grated ginger
- 1 tsp rice vinegar
- 1 chopped green onion
- Toasted sesame seeds

Directions:

1. Set air fryer to 125°C
2. Place eggs in the air fryer and cook for 15 minutes
3. Remove from the air fryer and place in a bowl of iced water for 10 minutes
4. Peel and cut in half
5. Scoop out the yolks and place in a food processor
6. Add the ingredients apart from the sesame seeds and green onion and combine until smooth
7. Place in a piping bag and pipe back into the egg whites
8. Garnish with seeds and green onion

Peppers With Aioli Dip

Servings: 4
Cooking Time:xx
Ingredients:

- 250g shishito peppers
- 2 tsp avocado oil
- 5 tbsp mayonnaise
- 2 tbsp lemon juice
- 1 minced clove of garlic
- 1 tbsp chopped parsley
- Salt and pepper for seasoning

Directions:

1. Take a medium bowl and combine the mayonnaise with the lemon juice, garlic, parsley and seasoning and create a smooth dip
2. Preheat the air fryer to 220°C
3. Toss the peppers in the oil and add to the air fryer
4. Cook for 4 minutes, until the peppers are soft and blistered on the outside
5. Remove and serve with the dip

Bacon Smokies

Servings: 8
Cooking Time:xx
Ingredients:

- 150g little smokies (pieces)
- 150g bacon
- 50g brown sugar
- Toothpicks

Directions:

1. Cut the bacon strips into thirds
2. Put the brown sugar into a bowl
3. Coat the bacon with the sugar

4. Wrap the bacon around the little smokies and secure with a toothpick
5. Heat the air fryer to 170°C
6. Place in the air fryer and cook for 10 minutes until crispy

Sweet Potato Crisps

Servings: 4
Cooking Time:xx
Ingredients:

- 1 sweet potato, peeled and thinly sliced
- 2 tbsp oil
- ¼ tsp salt
- ¼ tsp pepper
- 1 tsp chopped rosemary
- Cooking spray

Directions:

1. Place all ingredients in a bowl and mix well
2. Place in the air fryer and cook at 175°C for about 15 minutes until crispy

Korean Chicken Wings

Servings: 2
Cooking Time:xx
Ingredients:

- 25ml soy sauce
- 40g brown sugar
- 2 tbsp hot pepper paste
- 1 tsp sesame oil
- ½ tsp ginger paste
- ½ tsp garlic paste
- 2 green onions, chopped
- 400g chicken wings
- 1 tbsp vegetable oil

Directions:

1. Preheat air fryer to 200°C
2. Place all ingredients apart from chicken wings and vegetable oil in a pan and simmer for about 4 minutes set aside
3. Massage the vegetable oil into the chicken wings
4. Place in the air fryer and cook for about 10 minutes
5. Turn and cook for a further 10 minutes
6. Coat the wings in the sauce and return to the air fryer
7. Cook for about 2 minutes

Italian Rice Balls

Servings: 2
Cooking Time:xx
Ingredients:

- 400g cooked rice
- 25g breadcrumbs, plus an extra 200g for breading
- 2 tbsp flour, plus an extra 2 tbsp for breading
- 1 tbsp cornstarch, plus an extra 3 tbsp for breading
- 1 chopped bell pepper
- 1 chopped onion
- 2 tbsp olive oil
- 1 tsp red chilli flakes
- 5 chopped mozzarella cheese sticks
- A little water for the breading
- Salt and pepper for seasoning

Directions:

1. Place the cooked rice into a bowl and mash with a fork. Place to one side
2. Take a saucepan and add the oil, salting the onion and peppers until they're both soft
3. Add the chilli flakes and a little salt and combine
4. Add the mixture to the mashed rice and combine
5. Add the 2 tbsp flour and 1 tbsp cornstarch, along with the 25g breadcrumbs and combine well
6. Use your hands to create balls with the mixture
7. Stuff a piece of the mozzarella inside the balls and form around it
8. Take a bowl and add the rest of the flour, corn starch and a little seasoning, with a small amount of water to create a thick batter
9. Take another bowl and add the rest of the breadcrumbs
10. Dip each rice ball into the batter and then the breadcrumbs
11. Preheat the air fryer to 220°C
12. Cook for 6 minutes, before shaking and cooking for another 6 minutes

Air-fried Pickles

Servings: 4
Cooking Time:xx
Ingredients:

- 1/2 cup mayonnaise
- 2 tsp sriracha sauce
- 1 jar dill pickle slices
- 1 egg
- 2 tbsp milk
- 50g flour
- 50g cornmeal
- ½ tsp seasoned salt
- ¼ tsp paprika
- ¼ tsp garlic powder
- ⅛ tsp pepper
- Cooking spray

Directions:

1. Mix the mayo and sriracha together in a bowl and set aside
2. Heat the air fryer to 200°C
3. Drain the pickles and pat dry
4. Mix egg and milk together, in another bowl mix all the remaining ingredients
5. Dip the pickles in the egg mix then in the flour mix
6. Spray the air fryer with cooking spray
7. Cook for about 4 minutes until crispy

Garlic Pizza Toast

Servings: 8
Cooking Time:xx
Ingredients:

- 1 pack garlic Texas toast, or 8 slices of bread topped with garlic butter
- 100g pizza sauce
- 50g pepperoni
- 100g grated cheese

Directions:

1. Top each piece of toast with pizza sauce
2. Add cheese and pepperoni
3. Heat air fryer to 190°C
4. Place in the air fryer and cook for 5 minutes

Jalapeño Poppers

Servings: 2
Cooking Time:xx
Ingredients:

- 10 jalapeños, halved and deseeded
- 100g cream cheese
- 50g parsley
- 150g breadcrumbs

Directions:

1. Mix 1/2 the breadcrumbs with the cream cheese
2. Add the parsley
3. Stuff the peppers with the cream cheese mix
4. Top the peppers with the remaining breadcrumbs
5. Heat the air fryer to 185°C
6. Place in the air fryer and cook for 6-8 minutes

Chicken & Bacon Parcels

Servings: 4
Cooking Time:xx
Ingredients:

- 2 chicken breasts, boneless and skinless
- 200ml BBQ sauce
- 7 slices of bacon, cut lengthwise into halves
- 2 tbsp brown sugar

Directions:

1. Preheat the air fryer to 220°C
2. Cut the chicken into strips, you should have 7 in total
3. Wrap two strips of the bacon around each piece of chicken
4. Brush the BBQ sauce over the top and sprinkle with the brown sugar
5. Place the chicken into the basket and cook for 5 minutes
6. Turn the chicken over and cook for another 5 minutes

Stuffed Mushrooms

Servings: 24
Cooking Time:xx
Ingredients:

- 24 mushrooms
- ½ pepper, sliced
- ½ diced onion
- 1 small carrot, diced
- 200g grated cheese
- 2 slices bacon, diced
- 100g sour cream

Directions:

1. Place the mushroom stems, pepper, onion, carrot and bacon in a pan and cook for about 5 minutes
2. Stir in cheese and sour cream, cook until well combined
3. Heat the air fryer to 175°C
4. Add stuffing to each of the mushrooms
5. Place in the air fryer and cook for 8 minutes

Beetroot Crisps

Servings: 2
Cooking Time:xx
Ingredients:

- 3 medium beetroots
- 2 tbsp oil
- Salt to taste

Directions:

1. Peel and thinly slice the beetroot
2. Coat with the oil and season with salt
3. Preheat the air fryer to 200°C
4. Place in the air fryer and cook for 12-18 minutes until crispy

Popcorn Tofu

Servings: 4
Cooking Time:xx
Ingredients:

- 400g firm tofu
- 100g chickpea flour
- 100g oatmeal
- 2 tbsp yeast
- 150ml milk
- 400g breadcrumbs
- 1 tsp garlic powder
- 1 tsp onion powder
- 1 tbsp dijon mustard
- ½ tsp salt
- ½ tsp pepper
- 2 tbsp vegetable bouillon

Directions:

1. Rip the tofu into pieces. Place the breadcrumbs into a bowl, in another bowl mix the remaining ingredients
2. Dip the tofu into the batter mix and then dip into the breadcrumbs
3. Heat the air fryer to 175°C

4. Place the tofu in the air fryer and cook for 12 minutes shaking halfway through

Corn Nuts

Servings: 8
Cooking Time:xx
Ingredients:

- 1 giant white corn
- 3 tbsp vegetable oil
- 2 tsp salt

Directions:

1. Place the corn in a large bowl, cover with water and sit for 8 hours
2. Drain, pat dry and air dry for 20 minutes
3. Preheat the air fryer to 200°C
4. Place in a bowl and coat with oil and salt
5. Cook in the air fryer for 10 minutes shake then cook for a further 10 minutes

Pao De Queijo

Servings: 20
Cooking Time:xx
Ingredients:

- 150g sweet starch
- 150g sour starch
- 50ml milk
- 25ml water
- 25ml olive oil
- 1 tsp salt
- 2 eggs
- 100g grated cheese
- 50g grated parmesan

Directions:

1. Preheat the air fryer to 170°C
2. Mix the starch together in a bowl until well mixed
3. Add olive oil, milk and water to a pan, bring to the boil and reduce the heat
4. Add the starch and mix until all the liquid is absorbed
5. Add the eggs and mix to a dough
6. Add the cheeses and mix well
7. Form the dough into balls
8. Line the air fryer with parchment paper
9. Bake in the air fryer for 8-10 minutes

Cheese Wontons

Servings: 8
Cooking Time:xx
Ingredients:

- 8 wonton wrappers
- 1 carton pimento cheese
- Small dish of water
- Cooking spray

Directions:

1. Place one tsp of cheese in the middle of each wonton wrapper
2. Brush the edges of each wonton wrapper with water
3. Fold over to create a triangle and seal
4. Heat the air fryer to 190°C
5. Spray the wontons with cooking spray
6. Place in the air fryer and cook for 3 minutes
7. Turnover and cook for a further 3 minutes

Lumpia

Servings: 16
Cooking Time:xx
Ingredients:

- 400g Italian sausage
- 1 sliced onion
- 1 chopped carrot
- 50g chopped water chestnuts
- Cooking spray
- 2 cloves minced, garlic
- 2 tbsp soy sauce
- ½ tsp salt
- ¼ tsp ground ginger
- 16 spring roll wrappers

Directions:

1. Cook sausage in a pan for about 5 minutes. Add green onions, onions, water chestnuts and carrot cook for 7 minutes
2. Add garlic and cook for a further 2 minutes
3. Add the soy sauce, salt and ginger, stir to mix well
4. Add filling to each spring roll wrapper.
5. Roll over the bottom and tuck in the sides, continue to roll up the spring roll
6. Spray with cooking spray and place in the air fryer
7. Cook at 200°C for 4 minutes turn and cook for a further 4 minutes

Tostones

Servings: 4
Cooking Time:xx
Ingredients:

- 2 unripe plantains
- Olive oil cooking spray
- 300ml of water
- Salt to taste

Directions:

1. Preheat the air fryer to 200°C
2. Slice the tips off the plantain
3. Cut the plantain into 1 inch chunks
4. Place in the air fryer spray with oil and cook for 5 minutes
5. Remove the plantain from the air fryer and smash to ½ inch pieces
6. Soak in a bowl of salted water
7. Remove from the water and return to the air fryer season with salt cook for 5 minutes
8. Turn and cook for another 5 minutes

Spicy Chickpeas

Servings: 4
Cooking Time:xx
Ingredients:

- 1 can chickpeas
- 1 tbsp yeast
- 1 tbsp olive oil
- 1 tsp paprika
- 1 tsp garlic powder
- ½ tsp salt
- Pinch cumin

Directions:

1. Preheat air fryer to 180°C
2. Combine all ingredients
3. Add to the air fryer and cook for 22 minutes tossing every 4 minutes until cooked

Mozzarella Sticks

Servings: 4
Cooking Time:xx
Ingredients:

- 60ml water
- 50g flour
- 5 tbsp cornstarch
- 1 tbsp cornmeal
- 1 tsp garlic powder
- ½ tsp salt
- 100g breadcrumbs
- ½ tsp pepper
- ½ tsp parsley
- ½ tsp onion powder
- ¼ tsp oregano
- ½ tsp basil
- 200g mozzarella cut into ½ inch strips

Directions:

1. Mix water, flour, cornstarch, cornmeal, garlic powder and salt in a bowl
2. Stir breadcrumbs, pepper, parsley, onion powder, oregano and basil together in another bowl
3. Dip the mozzarella sticks in the batter then coat in the breadcrumbs
4. Heat the air fryer to 200°C
5. Cook for 6 minutes turn and cook for another 6 minutes

Onion Bahji

Servings: 8
Cooking Time:xx
Ingredients:

- 1 sliced red onion
- 1 sliced onion
- 1 tsp salt
- 1 minced jalapeño pepper
- 150g chickpea flour
- 4 tbsp water
- 1 clove garlic, minced
- 1 tsp coriander
- 1 tsp chilli powder
- 1 tsp turmeric
- ½ tsp cumin

Directions:

1. Place all ingredients in a bowl and mix well, leave to rest for 10 minutes
2. Preheat air fryer to 175°C
3. Spray air fryer with cooking spray.
4. Form mix into bahji shapes and add to air fryer
5. Cook for 6 minutes turn and cook for a further 6 minutes

Onion Pakoda

Servings: 2
Cooking Time:xx
Ingredients:

- 200g gram flour
- 2 onions, thinly sliced
- 1 tbsp crushed coriander seeds
- 1 tsp chilli powder
- ¾ tsp salt
- ¼ tsp turmeric
- ¼ tsp baking soda

Directions:

1. Mix all the ingredients together in a large bowl
2. Make bite sized pakodas
3. Heat the air fryer to 200ºC
4. Line the air fryer with foil
5. Place the pakoda in the air fryer and cook for 5 minutes
6. Turn over and cook for a further 5 minutes

Focaccia Bread

Servings: 8
Cooking Time:xx
Ingredients:

- 500g pizza dough
- 3 tbsp olive oil
- 2-3 garlic cloves, chopped
- ¼ tsp red pepper flakes
- 50g parsley
- 1 tsp basil
- 100g chopped red peppers
- 60g black olives halved
- 60g green olives halved
- Salt and pepper to taste

Directions:

1. Preheat the air fryer to 180ºC, make indentations in the pizza dough with your finger tips and set aside
2. Heat the olive oil in a pan add the garlic and cook for a few minutes, add the remaining ingredients and cook for another 5-8 minutes not letting the oil get too hot
3. Spread the oil mix over the dough with a spatula
4. Place in the air fryer and cook for 12-15 minutes

Thai Bites

Servings: 4
Cooking Time:xx
Ingredients:

- 400g pork mince
- 1 onion
- 1 tsp garlic paste
- 1 tbsp soy
- 1 tbsp Worcester sauce
- Salt and pepper
- 2 tsp Thai curry paste
- ½ lime juice and zest
- 1 tsp mixed spice
- 1 tsp Chinese spice
- 1 tsp coriander

Directions:

1. Place all ingredients in a bowl and mix well
2. Shape into balls
3. Place in the air fryer and cook at 180ºC for 15 minutes

Pepperoni Bread

Servings: 4
Cooking Time:xx
Ingredients:

- Cooking spray
- 400g pizza dough
- 200g pepperoni
- 1 tbsp dried oregano
- Ground pepper to taste
- Garlic salt to taste
- 1 tsp melted butter
- 1 tsp grated parmesan
- 50g grated mozzarella

Directions:

1. Line a baking tin with 2 inch sides with foil to fit in the air fryer
2. Spray with cooking spray
3. Preheat the air fryer to 200ºC
4. Roll the pizza dough into 1 inch balls and line the baking tin
5. Sprinkle with pepperoni, oregano, pepper and garlic salt
6. Brush with melted butter and sprinkle with parmesan
7. Place in the air fryer and cook for 15 minutes
8. Sprinkle with mozzarella and cook for another 2 minutes

Vegetarian & Vegan Recipes

Air Fryer Cheese Sandwich

Servings:2
Cooking Time:10 Minutes
Ingredients:
- 4 slices white or wholemeal bread
- 2 tbsp butter
- 50 g / 3.5 oz cheddar cheese, grated

Directions:
1. Preheat the air fryer to 180 °C / 350 °F and line the bottom of the basket with parchment paper.
2. Lay the slices of bread out on a clean surface and butter one side of each. Evenly sprinkle the cheese on two of the slices and cover with the final two slices.
3. Transfer the sandwiches to the air fryer, close the lid, and cook for 5 minutes until the bread is crispy and golden, and the cheese is melted.

Two-step Pizza

Servings: 1
Cooking Time:xx
Ingredients:
- BASE
- 130 g/generous ½ cup Greek yogurt
- 125 g self-raising/self-rising flour, plus extra for dusting
- ¼ teaspoon salt
- PIZZA SAUCE
- 100 g/3½ oz. passata/strained tomatoes
- 1 teaspoon dried oregano
- ¼ teaspoon garlic salt
- TOPPINGS
- 75 g/2½ oz. mozzarella, torn
- fresh basil leaves, to garnish

Directions:
1. Mix together the base ingredients in a bowl. Once the mixture starts to look crumbly, use your hands to bring the dough together into a ball. Transfer to a piece of floured parchment paper and roll to about 5 mm/¼ in. thick. Transfer to a second piece of non-floured parchment paper.
2. Preheat the air-fryer to 200°C/400°F.
3. Meanwhile, mix the pizza sauce ingredients together in a small bowl and set aside.

4. Prick the pizza base all over with a fork and transfer (on the parchment paper) to the preheated air-fryer and air-fry for 5 minutes. Turn the pizza base over and top with the pizza sauce and the torn mozzarella. Cook for a further 3–4 minutes, until the cheese has melted. Serve immediately with the basil scattered over the top.

Roasted Cauliflower

Servings: 2
Cooking Time:xx
Ingredients:
- 3 cloves garlic
- 1 tbsp peanut oil
- ½ tsp salt
- ½ tsp paprika
- 400g cauliflower florets

Directions:
1. Preheat air fryer to 200°C
2. Crush the garlic, place all ingredients in a bowl and mix well
3. Place in the air fryer and cook for about 15 minutes, shaking every 5 minutes

Vegetarian "chicken" Tenders

Servings: 4
Cooking Time:xx
Ingredients:
- 250g flour
- 3 eggs
- 100g panko bread crumbs
- 1 tsp garlic powder
- 2 packs of vegetarian chicken breasts
- ¾ tsp paprika
- ½ tsp cayenne
- ½ tsp pepper
- ½ tsp chilli powder
- ½ tsp salt

Directions:
1. Pour flour onto a plate, beat eggs into a bowl. Combine all remaining dry ingredients in a bowl
2. Cut the chicken into strips
3. Dip the chicken in flour, then egg and then into the breadcrumb mix

4. Heat the air fryer to 260°C
5. Cook for 6 minutes turn and then cook for another 6 minutes until golden brown

Roast Vegetables

Servings: 4
Cooking Time:xx
Ingredients:

- 100g diced courgette
- 100g diced squash
- 100g diced mushrooms
- 100g diced cauliflower
- 100g diced asparagus
- 100g diced pepper
- 2 tsp oil
- ½ tsp salt
- ¼ tsp pepper
- ¼ tsp seasoning

Directions:

1. Preheat air fryer to 180°C
2. Mix all ingredients together
3. Add to air fryer and cook for 10 minutes stirring halfway

Rainbow Vegetables

Servings: 4
Cooking Time:xx
Ingredients:

- 1 red pepper, cut into slices
- 1 squash sliced
- 1 courgette sliced
- 1 tbsp olive oil
- 150g sliced mushrooms
- 1 onion sliced
- Salt and pepper to taste

Directions:

1. Preheat air fryer to 180°C
2. Place all ingredients in a bowl and mix well
3. Place in the air fryer and cook for about 20 minutes turning halfway

Saganaki

Servings: 2
Cooking Time:xx
Ingredients:

- 200 g/7 oz. kefalotyri or manouri cheese, sliced into wedges 1 cm/½ in. thick
- 2 tablespoons plain/all-purpose flour
- olive oil, for drizzling

Directions:

1. Preheat the air-fryer to 200°C/400°F.
2. Dip each wedge of cheese in the flour, then tap off any excess. Drizzle olive oil onto both sides of the cheese slices
3. Add the cheese to the preheated air-fryer and air-fry for 3 minutes. Remove from the air-fryer and serve.

Aubergine Parmigiana

Servings: 2 As A Main Or 4 As A Side
Cooking Time:xx
Ingredients:

- 2 small or 1 large aubergine/eggplant, sliced 5 mm/¼ in. thick
- 1 tablespoon olive oil
- ¾ teaspoon salt
- 200 g/7 oz. mozzarella, sliced
- ½ teaspoon freshly ground black pepper
- 20 g/¼ cup finely grated Parmesan
- green vegetables, to serve
- SAUCE
- 135 g/5 oz. passata/strained tomatoes
- 1 teaspoon dried oregano
- ¼ teaspoon garlic salt
- 1 tablespoon olive oil

Directions:

1. Preheat the air-fryer to 200°C/400°F.
2. Rub each of the aubergine/eggplant slices with olive oil and salt. Divide the slices into two batches. Place one batch of the aubergine slices in the preheated air-fryer and air-fry for 4 minutes on one side, then turn over and air-fry for 2 minutes on the other side. Lay these on the base of a gratin dish that fits into your air-fryer.
3. Air-fry the second batch of aubergine slices in the same way. Whilst they're cooking, mix together the sauce ingredients in a small bowl.
4. Spread the sauce over the aubergines in the gratin dish. Add a layer of the mozzarella slices, then season with pepper. Add a second layer of aubergine slices, then top with Parmesan.
5. Place the gratin dish in the air-fryer and air-fry for 6 minutes, until the mozzarella is melted and the top of the dish is golden brown. Serve immediately with green vegetables on the side.

Broccoli Cheese

Servings: 2
Cooking Time:xx
Ingredients:

- 250g broccoli
- Cooking spray
- 10 tbsp evaporated milk
- 300g Mexican cheese
- 4 tsp Amarillo paste
- 6 saltine crackers

Directions:

1. Heat the air fryer to 190°C
2. Place the broccoli in the air fryer spray with cooking oil and cook for about 6 minutes
3. Place the remaining ingredients in a blender and process until smooth
4. Place in a bowl and microwave for 30 seconds
5. Pour over the broccoli and serve

Pakoras

Servings: 8
Cooking Time:xx
Ingredients:

- 200g chopped cauliflower
- 100g diced pepper
- 250g chickpea flour
- 30ml water
- ½ tsp cumin
- Cooking spray
- 1 onion, diced
- 1 tsp salt
- 1 garlic clove, minced
- 1 tsp curry powder
- 1 tsp coriander
- ½ tsp cayenne

Directions:

1. Preheat air fryer to 175°C
2. Place all ingredients in a bowl and mix well
3. Spray cooking basket with oil
4. Spoon 2 tbsp of mix into the basket and flatten, continue until the basket is full
5. Cook for 8 minutes, turn then cook for a further 8 minutes

Whole Wheat Pizza

Servings: 2
Cooking Time:xx
Ingredients:

- 100g marinara sauce
- 2 whole wheat pitta
- 200g baby spinach leaves
- 1 small plum tomato, sliced
- 1 clove garlic, sliced
- 400g grated cheese
- 50g shaved parmesan

Directions:

1. Preheat air fryer to 160°C
2. Spread each of the pitta with marinara sauce
3. Sprinkle with cheese, top with spinach, plum tomato and garlic. Finish with parmesan shavings
4. Place in the air fryer and cook for about 4 mins cheese has melted

Radish Hash Browns

Servings: 4
Cooking Time:xx
Ingredients:

- 300g radish
- 1 onion
- 1 tsp onion powder
- ¾ tsp sea salt
- ½ tsp paprika
- ¼ tsp ground black pepper
- 1 tsp coconut oil

Directions:

1. Wash the radish, trim off the roots and slice in a processor along with the onions
2. Add the coconut oil and mix well
3. Put the onions and radish into the air fryer and cook at 180°C for 8 minutes shaking a few times
4. Put the onion and radish in a bowl add seasoning and mix well
5. Put back in the air fryer and cook at 200°C for 5 minutes

Camembert & Soldiers

Servings: 2
Cooking Time:xx
Ingredients:

- 1 piece of Camembert
- 2 slices sandwich bread
- 1 tbsp mustard

Directions:

1. Preheat the air fryer to 180ºC
2. Place the camembert in a sturdy container, cook in the air fryer for 15 minutes
3. Toast the bread and cut into soldiers
4. Serve with the mustard by the side

Aubergine Dip

Servings: 4
Cooking Time:xx
Ingredients:

- 1 aubergine
- 2 tsp oil
- 3 tbsp tahini
- 1 tbsp lemon juice
- 1 clove garlic minced
- ⅛ tsp cumin
- ¼ tsp smoked salt
- ⅛ tsp salt
- Drizzle olive oil

Directions:

1. Cut the aubergine in half length wise and coat in oil, Place in the air fryer and cook at 200ºC for 20 minutes
2. Remove from the air fryer and allow to cool
3. Scoop out the aubergine from the peel and put in a food processor
4. Add all the remaining ingredients, blend to combine but not to a puree
5. Serve with a drizzle of olive oil

Artichoke Crostini

Servings: 2
Cooking Time:xx
Ingredients:

- 100g cashews
- 1 tbsp olive oil
- 1 tbsp lemon juice
- 1 tsp balsamic vinegar
- 3 tbsp hummus
- 200g grilled artichoke hearts

- ½ tsp basil
- ½ tsp oregano
- ⅛ tsp onion powder
- 1 clove garlic minced
- Salt
- 1 baguette cut in ½ inch slices

Directions:

1. Combine cashews, olive oil, lemon juice, balsamic vinegar, basil oregano, onion powder, garlic and salt in a bowl. Set aside
2. Place the baguette slices in the air fryer and cook at 180ºC for 3-4 minutes
3. Sprinkle the baguette slices with cashew mix then add the artichoke hearts
4. Serve with hummus

Flat Mushroom Pizzas

Servings: 1
Cooking Time:xx
Ingredients:

- 2 portobello mushrooms, cleaned and stalk removed
- 6 mozzarella balls
- 1 teaspoon olive oil
- PIZZA SAUCE
- 100 g/3½ oz. passata/strained tomatoes
- 1 teaspoon dried oregano
- ¼ teaspoon garlic salt

Directions:

1. Preheat the air-fryer to 180ºC/350ºF.
2. Mix the ingredients for the pizza sauce together in a small bowl. Fill each upturned portobello mushroom with sauce, then top each with three mozzarella balls and drizzle the olive oil over.
3. Add the mushrooms to the preheated air-fryer and air-fry for 8 minutes. Serve immediately.

Arancini

Servings: 12
Cooking Time:xx
Ingredients:
- 1 batch of risotto
- 100g panko breadcrumbs
- 1 tsp onion powder
- Salt and pepper
- 300ml warm marinara sauce

Directions:
1. Take ¼ cup risotto and form a rice ball
2. Mix the panko crumbs, onion powder, salt and pepper
3. Coat the risotto ball in the crumb mix
4. Place in the air fryer, spray with oil and cook at 200ºC for 10 minutes
5. Serve with marinara sauce

Roast Cauliflower & Broccoli

Servings: 6
Cooking Time:xx
Ingredients:
- 300g broccoli
- 300g cauliflower
- 2 tbsp oil
- ½ tsp garlic powder
- ¼ tsp salt
- ¼ tsp paprika
- ⅛ tsp pepper

Directions:
1. Preheat air fryer to 200ºC
2. Place broccoli and cauliflower in a bowl and microwave for 3 minutes
3. Add remaining ingredients and mix well
4. Add to the air fryer and cook for about 12 mins

Mini Quiche

Servings: 2
Cooking Time:xx
Ingredients:
- 100g raw cashews
- 3 tbsp milk
- ½ tsp hot sauce
- 1 tsp white miso paste
- 1 tsp mustard
- 300g tofu
- 100g bacon pieces
- 1 chopped red pepper
- 1 chopped onion
- 6 tbsp yeast
- ½ tsp onion powder
- ½ tsp paprika
- ½ tsp cumin
- ½ tsp chilli powder
- ½ tsp black pepper
- ⅛ tsp turmeric
- ½ tsp canola oil
- 50g curly kale

Directions:
1. Heat the oil in a pan, add the bacon pepper, onion and curly kale and cook for about 3 minutes
2. Place all the other ingredients into a blender and blend until smooth
3. Add to a bowl with the bacon, pepper, onion and curly kale and mix well
4. Fill silicone muffin cups with the mix
5. Place in the air fryer and cook at 165ºC for 15 minutes

Spring Ratatouille

Servings:2
Cooking Time:15 Minutes
Ingredients:
- 1 tbsp olive oil
- 4 Roma tomatoes, sliced
- 2 cloves garlic, minced
- 1 courgette, cut into chunks
- 1 red pepper and 1 yellow pepper, cut into chunks
- 2 tbsp mixed herbs
- 1 tbsp vinegar

Directions:
1. Preheat the air fryer to 190 ºC / 370 ºF and line the air fryer with parchment paper or grease it with olive oil.
2. Place all of the ingredients into a large mixing bowl and mix until fully combined.
3. Transfer the vegetables into the lined air fryer basket, close the lid, and cook for 15 minutes until the vegetables have softened.

Courgette Meatballs

Servings: 4
Cooking Time:xx
Ingredients:

- 400g oats
- 40g feta, crumbled
- 1 beaten egg
- Salt and pepper
- 150g courgette
- 1 tsp lemon rind
- 6 basil leaves, thinly sliced
- 1 tsp dill
- 1 tsp oregano

Directions:

1. Preheat the air fryer to 200°C
2. Grate the courgette into a bowl, squeeze any access water out
3. Add all the remaining ingredients apart from the oats and mix well
4. Blend the oats until they resemble breadcrumbs
5. Add the oats into the other mix and stir well
6. Form into balls and place in the air fryer cook for 10 minutes

Baked Aubergine Slices With Yogurt Dressing

Servings: 2
Cooking Time:xx
Ingredients:

- 1 aubergine/eggplant, sliced 1.5 cm/⅝ in. thick
- 3 tablespoons olive oil
- ½ teaspoon salt
- YOGURT DRESSING
- 1 small garlic clove
- 1 tablespoon tahini or nut butter
- 100 g/½ cup Greek yogurt
- 2 teaspoons freshly squeezed lemon juice
- 1 tablespoon runny honey
- a pinch of salt
- a pinch of ground cumin
- a pinch of sumac
- TO SERVE
- 30 g/1 oz. rocket/arugula
- 2 tablespoons freshly chopped mint
- 3 tablespoons pomegranate seeds

Directions:

1. Preheat the air-fryer to 180°C/350°F.
2. Drizzle the olive oil over each side of the aubergine/eggplant slices. Sprinkle with salt. Add the aubergines to the preheated air-fryer and air-fry for 10 minutes, turning halfway through cooking.
3. Meanwhile, make the dressing by combining all the ingredients in a mini food processor (alterantively, finely chop the garlic, add to a jar with the other ingredients and shake vigorously).
4. Serve the cooked aubergine slices on a bed of rocket/arugula, drizzled with the dressing and with the mint and pomegranate seeds scattered over the top.

Sweet Potato Taquitos

Servings: 10
Cooking Time:xx
Ingredients:

- 1 sweet potato cut into ½ inch pieces
- 1 ½ tsp oil
- 1 chopped onion
- 1 tsp minced garlic
- 400g black beans
- 3 tbsp water
- 10 corn tortillas
- 1 chipotle pepper, chopped
- ½ tsp cumin
- ½ tsp paprika
- ½ chilli powder
- ⅛ tsp salt
- ½ tsp maple syrup

Directions:

1. Place the sweet potato in the air fryer spray with oil and cook for 12 minutes at 200°C
2. Heat oil in a pan, add the onion and garlic and cook for a few minutes until soft
3. Add remaining ingredients to the pan, add 2 tbsp of water and combine
4. Add the sweet potato and 1 tbsp of water and mix
5. Warm the tortilla in the microwave for about 1 minute
6. Place a row of filling across the centre of each tortilla. Fold up the bottom of the tortilla, tuck under the filling, fold in the edges then continue to roll the tortilla
7. Place in the air fryer and cook for about 12 minutes

Ratatouille

Servings: 4
Cooking Time:xx
Ingredients:

- ½ small aubergine, cubed
- 1 courgette, cubed
- 1 tomato, cubed
- 1 pepper, cut into cubes
- ½ onion, diced
- 1 fresh cayenne pepper, sliced
- 1 tsp vinegar
- 5 sprigs basil, chopped
- 2 sprigs oregano, chopped
- 1 clove garlic, crushed
- Salt and pepper
- 1 tbsp olive oil
- 1 tbsp white wine

Directions:

1. Preheat air fryer to 200°C
2. Place all ingredients in a bowl and mix
3. Pour into a baking dish
4. Add dish to the air fryer and cook for 8 minutes, stir then cook for another 10 minutes

Cheese, Tomato & Pesto Crustless Quiches

Servings: 1–2
Cooking Time:xx
Ingredients:

- 40 g/½ cup grated mature Cheddar
- 3 eggs, beaten
- 3 cherry tomatoes, finely chopped
- salt and freshly ground black pepper
- ½ teaspoon olive oil, to grease ramekins
- 2 tablespoons pesto (jarred or see page 80)

Directions:

1. Preheat the air-fryer to 180°C/350°F.
2. Mix together the cheese, eggs, tomatoes, salt and pepper in a bowl.
3. Grease the ramekins with the oil (and line with parchment paper if you wish to remove the quiches to serve). Pour the egg mixture into the ramekins.
4. Place the ramekins in the preheated air-fryer and air-fry for 10 minutes, stirring the contents of the ramekins halfway through cooking. Serve hot with 1 tablespoon pesto drizzled over each quiche.

Roasted Garlic

Servings: 2
Cooking Time:xx
Ingredients:

- 1 head of garlic
- Drizzle of olive oil
- Salt and pepper for seasoning

Directions:

1. Remove paper peel from garlic
2. Place in foil and drizzle with oil
3. Place in the air fryer and cook at 200°C for 20 minutes
4. Season before serving

Artichoke Pasta

Servings: 2
Cooking Time:xx
Ingredients:

- 100g pasta
- 50g basil leaves
- 6 artichoke hearts
- 2 tbsp pumpkin seeds
- 2 tbsp lemon juice
- 1 clove garlic
- ½ tsp white miso paste
- 1 can chickpeas
- 1 tsp olive oil

Directions:

1. Place the chickpeas in the air fryer and cook at 200°C for 12 minutes
2. Cook the pasta according to packet instructions
3. Add the remaining ingredients to a food processor and blend
4. Add the pasta to a bowl and spoon over the pesto mix
5. Serve and top with roasted chickpeas

Ravioli Air Fryer Style

Servings: 4
Cooking Time:xx
Ingredients:

- Half a pack of frozen ravioli
- 200g Italian breadcrumbs
- 200ml buttermilk
- 5 tbsp marinara sauce
- 1 tbsp olive oil

Directions:

1. Preheat the air fryer to 220ºC
2. Place the buttermilk in a bowl
3. Add the breadcrumbs to another bowl
4. Take each piece of ravioli and dip it first into the buttermilk and then into the breadcrumbs, coating evenly
5. Add the ravioli to the air fryer and cook for 7 minutes, adding a small amount of oil at the halfway point
6. Serve with the marinara sauce on the side

Chickpea Falafel

Servings: 2
Cooking Time:xx
Ingredients:

- 400-g/14-oz can chickpeas, drained and rinsed
- 3 tablespoons freshly chopped coriander/cilantro
- 1 plump garlic clove, chopped
- freshly squeezed juice of ½ a lemon
- 1 teaspoon ground cumin
- 1 teaspoon smoked paprika
- 1 teaspoon salt
- 2 teaspoons olive oil (plus extra in a spray bottle or simply drizzle over)
- ½ teaspoon chilli/hot red pepper flakes

Directions:

1. In a food processor combine all the ingredients except the chilli/hot red pepper flakes. Divide the mixture into 6 equal portions and mould into patties.
2. Preheat the air-fryer to 180ºC/350ºF.
3. Spray each falafel with extra olive oil and sprinkle with chilli/hot red pepper flakes, then place in the preheated air-fryer and air-fry for 7 minutes, or until just brown on top. Remove carefully and serve.

Jackfruit Taquitos

Servings: 2
Cooking Time:xx
Ingredients:

- 1 large Jackfruit
- 250g red beans
- 100g pico de gallo sauce
- 50ml water
- 2 tbsp water
- 4 wheat tortillas
- Olive oil spray

Directions:

1. Place the jackfruit, red beans, sauce and water in a saucepan
2. Bring to the boil and simmer for 25 minutes
3. Preheat the air fryer to 185ºC
4. Mash the jackfruit mixture, add ¼ cup of the mix to each tortilla and roll up tightly
5. Spray with olive oil and place in the air fryer
6. Cook for 8 minutes

Crispy Potato Peels

Servings: 1
Cooking Time:xx
Ingredients:

- Peels from 4 potatoes
- Cooking spray
- Salt to season

Directions:

1. Heat the air fryer to 200ºC
2. Place the peels in the air fryer spray with oil and sprinkle with salt
3. Cook for about 6-8 minutes until crispy

Bagel Pizza

Servings: 1
Cooking Time:xx
Ingredients:

- 1 bagel
- 2 tbsp marinara sauce
- 6 slices vegan pepperoni
- 2 tbsp mozzarella
- Pinch of basil

Directions:

1. Heat the air fryer to 180ºC
2. Cut the bagel in half and toast for 2 minutes in the air fryer
3. Remove from the air fryer and top with marinara sauce, pepperoni and mozzarella

4. Return to the air fryer and cook for 4-5 minutes
5. Sprinkle with basil to serve

Shakshuka

Servings: 2
Cooking Time:xx
Ingredients:

- 2 eggs
- BASE
- 100 g/3½ oz. thinly sliced (bell) peppers
- 1 red onion, halved and thinly sliced
- 2 medium tomatoes, chopped
- 2 teaspoons olive oil
- ¼ teaspoon salt
- ¼ teaspoon freshly ground black pepper
- ½ teaspoon chilli/hot red pepper flakes
- SAUCE
- 100 g/3½ oz. passata/strained tomatoes
- 1 tablespoon tomato purée/paste
- 1 teaspoon balsamic vinegar
- ½ teaspoon runny honey
- ½ teaspoon ground cumin
- ½ teaspoon paprika
- ¼ teaspoon salt
- ⅛ teaspoon freshly ground black pepper

Directions:

1. Preheat the air-fryer to 180°C/350°F.
2. Combine the base ingredients together in a baking dish that fits inside your air-fryer. Add the dish to the preheated air-fryer and air-fry for 10 minutes, stirring halfway through cooking.
3. Meanwhile, combine the sauce ingredients in a bowl. Pour this into the baking dish when the 10 minutes are up. Stir, then make a couple of wells in the sauce for the eggs. Crack the eggs into the wells, then cook for a further 5 minutes or until the eggs are just cooked and yolks still runny. Remove from the air-fryer and serve.

Miso Mushrooms On Sourdough Toast

Servings: 1
Cooking Time:xx
Ingredients:

- 1 teaspoon miso paste
- 1 teaspoon oil, such as avocado or coconut (melted)
- 1 teaspoon soy sauce
- 80 g/3 oz. chestnut mushrooms, sliced 5 mm/½ in. thick
- 1 large slice sourdough bread
- 2 teaspoons butter or plant-based spread
- a little freshly chopped flat-leaf parsley, to serve

Directions:

1. Preheat the air-fryer to 200°C/400°F.
2. In a small bowl or ramekin mix together the miso paste, oil and soy sauce.
3. Place the mushrooms in a small shallow gratin dish that fits inside your air-fryer. Add the sauce to the mushrooms and mix together. Place the gratin dish in the preheated air-fryer and air-fry for 6–7 minutes, stirring once during cooking.
4. With 4 minutes left to cook, add the bread to the air-fryer and turn over at 2 minutes whilst giving the mushrooms a final stir.
5. Once cooked, butter the toast and serve the mushrooms on top, scattered with chopped parsley.

Potato Gratin

Servings: 4
Cooking Time:xx
Ingredients:

- 2 large potatoes
- 2 beaten eggs
- 100ml coconut cream
- 1 tbsp plain flour
- 50g grated cheddar

Directions:

1. Slice the potatoes into thin slices, place in the air fryer and cook for 10 minutes at 180°C
2. Mix eggs, coconut cream and flour together
3. Line four ramekins with the potato slices
4. Cover with the cream mixture, sprinkle with cheese and cook for 10 minutes at 200°C

Vegan Fried Ravioli

Servings: 4
Cooking Time:xx
Ingredients:

- 100g panko breadcrumbs
- 2 tsp yeast
- 1 tsp basil
- 1 tsp oregano
- 1 tsp garlic powder
- Pinch salt and pepper
- 50ml liquid from can of chickpeas
- 150g vegan ravioli
- Cooking spray
- 50g marinara for dipping

Directions:

1. Combine the breadcrumbs, yeast, basil, oregano, garlic powder and salt and pepper
2. Put the liquid from the chickpeas in a bowl
3. Dip the ravioli in the liquid then dip into the breadcrumb mix
4. Heat the air fryer to 190°C
5. Place the ravioli in the air fryer and cook for about 6 minutes until crispy

Stuffed Peppers

Servings: 6
Cooking Time:xx
Ingredients:

- 250g diced potatoes
- 100g peas
- 1 small onion, diced
- 1 carrot, diced
- 1 bread roll, diced
- 2 garlic cloves, minced
- 2 tsp mixed herbs
- 6 bell peppers
- 100g grated cheese

Directions:

1. Preheat air fryer to 180°C
2. Combine all the ingredients together apart from the peppers
3. Stuff the peppers with the mix
4. Place in the air fryer and cook for about 20 minutes

Tempura Veggies

Servings: 4
Cooking Time:xx

Ingredients:

- 150g flour
- ½ tsp salt
- ½ tsp pepper
- 2 eggs
- 2 tbsp cup water
- 100g avocado wedges
- 100g courgette slices
- 100g panko breadcrumbs
- 2 tsp oil
- 100g green beans
- 100g asparagus spears
- 100g red onion rings
- 100g pepper rings

Directions:

1. Mix together flour, salt and pepper. In another bowl mix eggs and water
2. Stir together panko crumbs and oil in a separate bowl
3. Dip vegetables in the flour mix, then egg and then the bread crumbs
4. Preheat the air fryer to 200°C
5. Place in the air fryer and cook for about 10 minutes until golden brown

Lentil Balls With Zingy Rice

Servings: 4
Cooking Time:xx
Ingredients:

- 2 cans lentils
- 200g walnut halves
- 3 tbsp dried mushrooms
- 3 tbsp parsley
- 1 ½ tbsp tomato paste
- ¾ tsp salt
- ½ tsp pepper
- 100g bread crumbs
- 400ml water
- 200g rice
- 2 tbsp lemon juice
- 2 tsp lemon zest
- Salt to taste

Directions:

1. Preheat air fryer to 190°C
2. Place the lentils, walnuts, mushrooms, parsley, tomato paste, salt, pepper in a food processor and blend
3. Fold in the bread crumbs

4. Form the mix into balls and place in the air fryer
5. Cook for 10 minutes turn then cook for a further 5 minutes
6. Add the rice to a pan with water, bring to the boil and simmer for 20 minutes
7. Stir in the lemon juice, lemon zest and salt. Serve

Courgette Burgers

Servings: 4
Cooking Time:xx
Ingredients:

- 1 courgette
- 1 small can of chickpeas, drained
- 3 spring onions
- Pinch of dried garlic
- Salt and pepper
- 3 tbsp coriander
- 1 tsp chilli powder
- 1 tsp mixed spice
- 1 tsp cumin

Directions:

1. Grate the courgette and drain the excess water
2. Thinly slice the spring onions and add to the bowl with the chickpeas, courgette and seasoning
3. Bind the ingredients and form into patties
4. Place in the air fryer and cook for 12 minutes at 200ºC

Spicy Spanish Potatoes

Servings: 2
Cooking Time:xx
Ingredients:

- 4 large potatoes
- 1 tbsp olive oil
- 2 tsp paprika
- 2 tsp dried garlic
- 1 tsp barbacoa seasoning
- Salt and pepper

Directions:

1. Chop the potatoes into wedges
2. Place them in a bowl with olive oil and seasoning, mix well
3. Add to the air fryer and cook at 160ºC for 20 minutes
4. Shake, increase heat to 200ºC and cook for another 3 minutes

Tomato And Herb Tofu

Servings:4
Cooking Time:10 Minutes
Ingredients:

- 1 x 400 g / 14 oz block firm tofu
- 1 tbsp soy sauce
- 2 tbsp tomato paste
- 1 tsp dried oregano
- 1 tsp dried basil
- 1 tsp garlic powder

Directions:

1. Remove the tofu from the packaging and place on a sheet of kitchen roll. Place another sheet of kitchen roll on top of the tofu and place a plate on top of it.
2. Use something heavy to press the plate down on top of the tofu. Leave for 10 minutes to press the water out of the tofu.
3. Remove the paper towels from the tofu and chop them into even slices that are around ½ cm thick.
4. Preheat the air fryer to 180 ºC / 350 ºF. Remove the mesh basket from the air fryer machine and line with parchment paper.
5. Place the tofu slices on a lined baking sheet.
6. In a bowl, mix the soy sauce, tomato paste, dried oregano, dried basil, and garlic powder until fully combined.
7. Spread the mixture evenly over the tofu slices. Place the tofu slices on the baking sheet in the lined air fryer basket and cook for 10 minutes until the tofu is firm and crispy.
8. Serve the tofu slices with a side of rice or noodles and some hot vegetables.

Chickpea And Sweetcorn Falafel

Servings:4
Cooking Time:15 Minutes
Ingredients:

- ½ onion, sliced
- 2 cloves garlic, peeled and sliced
- 2 tbsp fresh parsley, chopped
- 2 tbsp fresh coriander, chopped
- 2 x 400 g / 14 oz chickpeas, drained and rinsed
- 1 tsp salt
- 1 tsp black pepper
- 1 tsp baking powder

- 1 tsp dried mixed herbs
- 1 tsp cumin
- 1 tsp chili powder
- 50 g / 1.8 oz sweetcorn, fresh or frozen

Directions:

1. Preheat the air fryer to 180 °C / 350 °F and line the bottom of the basket with parchment paper.
2. In a food processor, place the onion, garlic cloves, fresh parsley, and fresh coriander. Pulse the ingredients in 30-second intervals until they form a smooth mixture. Scrape the mixture from the sides of the food processor in between each interval if necessary.
3. Mix in the chickpeas, salt, black pepper, baking powder, dried mixed herbs, cumin, and chili powder. Pulse the mixture until fully combined and smooth. Add more water if the mixture is looking a bit dry. The mixture should be dry but not crumbly.
4. Use a spoon to scoop out 2 tbsp of the chickpea mixture at a time and roll into small, even falafels.
5. Transfer the falafels into the prepared air fryer basket and cook for 12-15 minutes.
6. Serve the falafels either hot or cold as a side dish to your main meal or as part of a large salad.

Spinach And Egg Air Fryer Breakfast Muffins

Servings:4
Cooking Time:10 Minutes

Ingredients:

- 8 eggs
- 100 g / 3.5 oz fresh spinach
- 50 g / 1.8 oz cheddar cheese, grated
- ½ onion, finely sliced
- 1 tsp black pepper

Directions:

1. Preheat your air fryer to 200 °C / 400 °F and line an 8-pan muffin tray with parchment paper or grease with olive oil.
2. Gently press the spinach leaves into the bottom of each prepared muffin cup.
3. Sprinkle the finely sliced onion on top of the spinach.
4. Crack 2 eggs into each cup on top of the spinach and add some of the grated cheddar

cheese on top of the eggs. Top with a light sprinkle of black pepper.
5. Carefully place the muffins into the air fryer basket and shut the lid. Bake for 10 minutes until the eggs are set and the muffins are hot throughout.
6. Serve the muffins while still hot for breakfast.

Quinoa-stuffed Romano Peppers

Servings: 2
Cooking Time:xx

Ingredients:

- 1 tablespoon olive oil
- 1 onion, diced
- 1 garlic clove, chopped
- 100 g/⅔ cup uncooked quinoa
- 1½ tablespoons fajita seasoning
- 140 g/1 cup canned sweetcorn/corn kernels (drained weight)
- 3 romano peppers, sliced lengthways, seeds removed but stalk left intact
- 60 g/⅔ cup grated mature Cheddar

Directions:

1. Heat the oil in a saucepan. Add the onion and garlic and sauté for 5 minutes, until soft. Add the quinoa, fajita seasoning and 250 ml/1 cup water. Bring to a simmer, then cover with a lid and simmer for 15 minutes or until the quinoa is cooked and the water absorbed. Stir in the sweetcorn/corn kernels. Stuff each pepper half with the quinoa mixture, then top with grated cheese.
2. Preheat the air-fryer to 180°C/350°F.
3. Place the peppers on an air-fryer liner or a piece of pierced parchment paper, place in the preheated air-fryer and air-fry for 12–14 minutes, depending how 'chargrilled' you like your peppers.

Baked Potato

Servings: 1
Cooking Time:xx
Ingredients:

- 1 large potato
- 1 tsp oil
- ¼ tsp onion powder
- ⅛ tsp coarse salt
- 1 tbsp of butter
- 1 tbsp of cream cheese
- 1 strip of bacon, diced
- 1 tbsp olives
- 1 tbsp chives

Directions:

1. Pierce the potato in several places with a fork, rub with oil, salt and onion powder
2. Place in the air fryer and cook at 200°C for 35-40 minutes
3. Remove from the air fryer, cut and top with the toppings

Parmesan Truffle Oil Fries

Servings: 2
Cooking Time:xx
Ingredients:

- 3 large potatoes, peeled and cut
- 2 tbsp truffle oil
- 2 tbsp grated parmesan
- 1 tsp paprika
- 1 tbsp parsley
- Salt and pepper to taste

Directions:

1. Coat the potatoes with truffle oil and sprinkle with seasonings
2. Add the fries to the air fryer
3. Cook at 180°C for about 15 minutes shake halfway through
4. Sprinkle with parmesan and parsley to serve

Roasted Vegetable Pasta

Servings:4
Cooking Time:15 Minutes
Ingredients:

- 400 g / 14 oz penne pasta
- 1 courgette, sliced
- 1 red pepper, deseeded and sliced
- 100 g / 3.5 oz mushroom, sliced
- 2 tbsp olive oil
- 1 tsp Italian seasoning
- 200 g cherry tomatoes, halved
- 2 tbsp fresh basil, chopped
- ½ tsp black pepper

Directions:

1. Cook the pasta according to the packet instructions.
2. Preheat the air fryer to 190 °C / 370 °F and line the air fryer with parchment paper or grease it with olive oil.
3. In a bowl, place the courgette, pepper, and mushroom, and toss in 2 tbsp olive oil
4. Place the vegetables in the air fryer and cook for 15 minutes.
5. Once the vegetables have softened, mix with the penne pasta, chopped cherry tomatoes, and fresh basil.
6. Serve while hot with a sprinkle of black pepper in each dish.

Satay Tofu Skewers

Servings: 2
Cooking Time:xx
Ingredients:

- 300 g/10½ oz. firm tofu
- Lime-Almond Satay Sauce (see page 87), to serve
- MARINADE
- 200 ml/¾ cup coconut milk (including the thick part from the can)
- 1 plump garlic clove, finely chopped
- 2 teaspoons grated ginger
- 2 tablespoons soy sauce
- 1 heaped tablespoon smooth peanut butter
- 1 tablespoon maple syrup
- 1 tablespoon mild curry powder
- 1 tablespoon fish sauce or plant-based alternative

Directions:

1. Cut the tofu into 2 x 2-cm/¾ x ¾-in. cubes. Mix the marinade ingredients thoroughly, then toss in the tofu cubes. Once the tofu cubes are covered in the marinade, leave in the fridge to marinate for at least 4 hours.
2. Preheat the air-fryer to 180°C/350°F.
3. Thread the tofu cubes onto 4 skewers that fit inside your air-fryer. Place on an air-fryer liner or a piece of pierced parchment paper and add

to the preheated air-fryer. Air-fry for 12 minutes, turning over once during cooking.

4. Serve the tofu skewers alongside a bowl of the Lime-Almond Satay Sauce.

Spinach And Feta Croissants

Servings:4
Cooking Time:10 Minutes
Ingredients:

- 4 pre-made croissants
- 100 g / 7 oz feta cheese, crumbled
- 1 tsp dried chives
- 1 tsp garlic powder
- 50 g / 3.5 oz fresh spinach, chopped

Directions:

1. Preheat the air fryer to 180 °C / 350 °F. Remove the mesh basket from the air fryer machine and line with parchment paper.
2. Cut the croissants in half and lay each half out on the lined mesh basket.
3. In a bowl, combine the crumbled feta cheese, dried chives, garlic powder, and chopped spinach until they form a consistent mixture.
4. Spoon some of the mixture one half of the four croissants and cover with the second half of the croissants to seal in the filling.
5. Carefully slide the croissants in the mesh basket into the air fryer machine, close the lid, and cook for 10 minutes until the pastry is crispy and the feta cheese has melted.

Desserts Recipes

Lemon Tarts

Servings: 8
Cooking Time:xx
Ingredients:

- 100g butter
- 225g plain flour
- 30g caster sugar
- Zest and juice of 1 lemon
- 4 tsp lemon curd

Directions:

1. In a bowl mix together butter, flour and sugar until it forms crumbs, add the lemon zest and juice
2. Add a little water at a time and mix to form a dough
3. Roll out the dough and line 8 small ramekins with it
4. Add ¼ tsp of lemon curd to each ramekin
5. Cook in the air fryer for 15 minutes at 180°C

Apple Fritters

Servings: 4
Cooking Time:xx
Ingredients:

- 225g self raising flour
- 200g greek yogurt
- 2 tsp sugar
- 1 tbsp cinnamon
- 1 apple peeled and chopped
- 225g icing sugar
- 2 tbsp milk

Directions:

1. Mix the flour, yogurt, sugar, cinnamon and apple together. Knead for about 3 -4 minutes
2. Mix the icing sugar and milk together to make the glaze and set aside
3. Line the air fryer with parchment paper and spray with cooking spray
4. Divide the fritter mix into four, flatten each portion and place in the air fryer
5. Cook at 185°C for about 15 minutes turning halfway
6. Drizzle with glaze to serve

Lemon Buns

Servings: 12
Cooking Time:xx
Ingredients:

- 100g butter
- 100g caster sugar
- 2 eggs
- 100g self raising flour
- ½ tsp vanilla essence
- 1 tsp cherries
- 50g butter
- 100g icing sugar
- ½ small lemon rind and juice

Directions:

1. Preheat the air fryer to 170ºC
2. Cream the 100g butter, sugar and vanilla together until light and fluffy
3. Beat in the eggs one at a time adding a little flour with each
4. Fold in the remaining flour
5. Half fill bun cases with the mix, place in the air fryer and cook for 8 minutes
6. Cream 50g butter then mix in the icing sugar, stir in the lemon
7. Slice the top off each bun and create a butterfly shape using the icing to hold together. Add a 1/3 cherry to each one

Granola Bars

Servings: 6
Cooking Time:xx
Ingredients:

- 250g oats
- 60g melted butter
- 30g sugar
- 3 tbsp honey
- Handful of raisins
- 1 apple cooked and peeled
- 1 tbsp olive oil
- 1 tsp vanilla
- 1 tsp cinnamon

Directions:

1. Add all the dry ingredients to the blender and mix
2. Add all the wet ingredients to the air fryer pan and mix well
3. Add the dry ingredients and mix well

4. Add the raisins and press down the mix into the pan
5. Cook for 10 mins at 160ºC then at 5 minutes for 180ºC
6. Chop into bars and serve

Cinnamon-maple Pineapple Kebabs

Servings: 2
Cooking Time:xx
Ingredients:

- 4 x pineapple strips, roughly 2 x 2 cm/¾ x ¾ in. by length of pineapple
- 1 teaspoon maple syrup
- ½ teaspoon vanilla extract
- ¼ teaspoon ground cinnamon
- Greek or plant-based yogurt and grated lime zest, to serve

Directions:

1. Line the air-fryer with an air-fryer liner or a piece of pierced parchment paper. Preheat the air-fryer to 180ºC/350ºF.
2. Stick small metal skewers through the pineapple lengthways. Mix the maple syrup and vanilla extract together, then drizzle over the pineapple and sprinkle over the cinnamon.
3. Add the skewers to the preheated lined air-fryer and air-fry for 15 minutes, turning once. If there is any maple-vanilla mixture left after the initial drizzle, then drizzle this over the pineapple during cooking too. Serve with yogurt and lime zest.

Fruit Crumble

Servings: 2
Cooking Time:xx
Ingredients:

- 1 diced apple
- 75g frozen blackberries
- 25g brown rice flour
- 2 tbsp sugar
- ½ tsp cinnamon
- 2 tbsp butter

Directions:

1. Preheat air fryer to 150ºC
2. Mix apple and blackberries in an air fryer safe baking pan
3. In a bowl mix the flour, sugar, cinnamon and butter, spoon over the fruit

4. Cook for 15 minutes

Baked Nectarines

Servings: 4
Cooking Time:xx
Ingredients:

- 2 teaspoons maple syrup
- 1 teaspoon vanilla extract
- 1 teaspoon ground cinnamon
- 4 nectarines, halved and stones/pits removed
- chopped nuts, yogurt and runny honey, to serve (optional)

Directions:

1. Preheat the air-fryer to 180°C/350° F.
2. Mix the maple syrup, vanilla extract and cinnamon in a ramekin or shake in a jar to combine. Lay the nectarine halves on an air-fryer liner or piece of pierced parchment paper. Drizzle over the maple syrup mix.
3. Place in the preheated air-fryer and air-fry for 9–11 minutes, until soft when pricked with a fork. Serve scattered with chopped nuts and with a generous dollop of yogurt. Drizzle over some honey if you wish.

Pumpkin Spiced Bread Pudding

Servings: 2
Cooking Time:xx
Ingredients:

- 175g heavy cream
- 500g pumpkin puree
- 30ml milk
- 25g sugar
- 1 large egg, plus one extra yolk
- ⅛ tsp salt
- ½ tsp pumpkin spice
- 500g cubed crusty bread
- 4 tbsp butter

Directions:

1. Place all of the ingredients apart from the bread and butter into a bowl and mix.
2. Add the bread and melted butter to the bowl and mix well
3. Heat the air fryer to 175°C
4. Pour the mix into a baking tin and cook in the air fryer for 35-40 minutes
5. Serve with maple cream

Apple And Cinnamon Puff Pastry Pies

Servings:8
Cooking Time:20 Minutes
Ingredients:

- 4 tbsp butter
- 4 tbsp white sugar
- 2 tbsp brown sugar
- 1 tsp cinnamon
- 1 tsp nutmeg
- 1 tsp salt
- 4 apples, peeled and diced
- 2 large sheets puff pastry
- 1 egg

Directions:

1. Preheat the air fryer to 180 °C / 350 °F. Remove the mesh basket from the machine and line it with parchment paper.
2. In a bowl, whisk together the butter, white sugar, brown sugar, cinnamon, nutmeg, and salt.
3. Place the apples in a heatproof baking dish and coat them in the butter and sugar mixture. Transfer to the air fryer and cook for 10 minutes.
4. Meanwhile, roll out the pastry on a clean, floured surface. Cut the sheets into 8 equal parts.
5. Once the apples are hot and softened, evenly spread the mixture between the pastry sheets. Fold the sheets over to cover the apple and gently press the edges using a fork or your fingers to seal the mixture in.
6. Beat the egg in a bowl and use a brush to coat the top of each pastry sheet.
7. Carefully transfer the filled pastry sheets to the prepared air fryer basket, close the lid, and cook for 10 minutes until the pastry is golden and crispy.

Butter Cake

Servings: 4
Cooking Time:xx
Ingredients:

- Cooking spray
- 7 tbsp butter
- 25g white sugar
- 2 tbsp white sugar
- 1 egg
- 300g flour
- Pinch salt
- 6 tbsp milk

Directions:

1. Preheat air fryer to 175°C
2. Spray a small fluted tube pan with cooking spray
3. Beat the butter and all of the sugar together in a bowl until creamy
4. Add the egg and mix until fluffy, add the salt and flour mix well. Add the milk and mix well
5. Put the mix in the pan and cook in the air fryer for 15 minutes

Chonut Holes

Servings: 12
Cooking Time:xx
Ingredients:

- 225g flour
- 75g sugar
- 1 tsp baking powder
- ¼ tsp cinnamon
- 2 tbsp sugar
- ½ tsp salt
- 2 tbsp aquafaba
- 1 tbsp melted coconut oil
- 75ml soy milk
- 2 tsp cinnamon

Directions:

1. In a bowl mix the flour, ¼ cup sugar, baking powder, ¼ tsp cinnamon and salt
2. Add the aquafaba, coconut oil and soy milk mix well
3. In another bowl mix 2 tsp cinnamon and 2 tbsp sugar
4. Line the air fryer with parchment paper
5. Divide the dough into 12 pieces and dredge with the cinnamon sugar mix

6. Place in the air fryer at 185°C and cook for 6-8 minutes, don't shake them

Chocolate Cake

Servings: 2
Cooking Time:xx
Ingredients:

- 3 eggs
- 75ml sour cream
- 225g flour
- 150g sugar
- 2 tsp vanilla extract
- 25g cocoa powder
- 1 tsp baking powder
- ½ tsp baking soda

Directions:

1. Preheat the air fryer to 160°C
2. Mix all the ingredients together in a bowl
3. Pour into a greased baking tin
4. Place into the air fryer and cook for 25 minutes
5. Allow to cool and ice with chocolate frosting

Chocolate Souffle

Servings:2
Cooking Time:15 Minutes
Ingredients:

- 2 eggs
- 4 tbsp brown sugar
- 1 tsp vanilla extract
- 4 tbsp butter, melted
- 4 tbsp milk chocolate chips
- 4 tbsp flour

Directions:

1. Preheat the air fryer to 180 °C / 350 °F. Remove the mesh basket from the machine and line it with parchment paper.
2. Separate the egg whites from the egg yolks and place them in two separate bowls.
3. Beat the yolks together with the brown sugar, vanilla extract, melted butter, milk chocolate chips, and flour in a bowl. It should form a smooth, consistent mixture.
4. Whisk the egg whites until they form stiff peaks. In batches, fold the egg whites into the chocolate mixture.
5. Divide the batter evenly between two souffle dishes and place them in the lined air fryer basket.

6. Cook the souffle dishes for 15 minutes until hot and set.

New York Cheesecake

Servings: 8
Cooking Time:xx
Ingredients:

- 225g plain flour
- 100g brown sugar
- 100g butter
- 50g melted butter
- 1 tbsp vanilla essence
- 750g soft cheese
- 2 cups caster sugar
- 3 large eggs
- 50ml quark

Directions:

1. Add the flour, sugar, and 100g butter to a bowl and mix until combined. Form into biscuit shapes place in the air fryer and cook for 15 minutes at 180°C
2. Grease a springform tin
3. Break the biscuits up and mix with the melted butter, press firmly into the tin
4. Mix the soft cheese and sugar in a bowl until creamy, add the eggs and vanilla and mix. Mix in the quark
5. Pour the cheesecake batter into the pan
6. Place in your air fryer and cook for 30 minutes at 180°C. Leave in the air fryer for 30 minutes whilst it cools
7. Refrigerate for 6 hours

Zebra Cake

Servings: 6
Cooking Time:xx
Ingredients:

- 115g butter
- 2 eggs
- 100g caster sugar
- 1 tbsp cocoa powder
- 100g self raising flour
- 30ml milk
- 1tsp vanilla

Directions:

1. Preheat air fryer to 160°C
2. Line a 6 inch baking tin
3. Beat together the butter and sugar until light and fluffy

4. Add eggs one at a time then add the vanilla and milk
5. Add the flour and mix well
6. Divide the mix in half
7. Add cocoa powder to half the mix and mix well
8. Add a scoop of each of the batters at a time until it's all in the tin, place in the air fryer and cook for 30 minutes

Christmas Biscuits

Servings: 8
Cooking Time:xx
Ingredients:

- 225g self raising flour
- 100g caster sugar
- 100g butter
- Juice and rind of orange
- 1 egg beaten
- 2 tbsp cocoa
- 2 tsp vanilla essence
- 8 pieces dark chocolate

Directions:

1. Preheat the air fryer to 180°C
2. Rub the butter into the flour. Add the sugar, vanilla, orange and cocoa mix well
3. Add the egg and mix to a dough
4. Split the dough into 8 equal pieces
5. Place a piece of chocolate in each piece of dough and form into a ball covering the chocolate
6. Place in the air fryer and cook for 15 minutes

Strawberry Danish

Servings: 2
Cooking Time:xx
Ingredients:

- 1 tube crescent roll dough
- 200g cream cheese
- 25g strawberry jam
- 50g diced strawberries
- 225g powdered sugar
- 2-3 tbsp cream

Directions:

1. Roll out the dough
2. Spread the cream cheese over the dough, cover in jam
3. Sprinkle with strawberries
4. Roll the dough up from the short side and pinch to seal

5. Line the air fryer with parchment paper and spray with cooking spray
6. Place the dough in the air fryer and cook at 175ºC for 20 minutes
7. Mix the cream with the powdered sugar and drizzle on top once cooked

Milk And White Chocolate Chip Air Fryer Donuts With Frosting

Servings:4
Cooking Time:10 Minutes
Ingredients:
- For the donuts:
- 200 ml milk (any kind)
- 50 g / 3.5 oz brown sugar
- 50 g / 3.5 oz granulated sugar
- 1 tbsp active dry yeast
- 2 tbsp olive oil
- 4 tbsp butter, melted
- 1 egg, beaten
- 1 tsp vanilla extract
- 400 g / 14 oz plain flour
- 4 tbsp cocoa powder
- 100 g / 3.5 oz milk chocolate chips
- For the frosting:
- 5 tbsp powdered sugar
- 2 tbsp cocoa powder
- 100 ml heavy cream
- 50 g / 1.8 oz white chocolate chips, melted

Directions:
1. To make the donuts, whisk together the milk, brown and granulated sugars, and active dry yeast in a bowl. Set aside for a few minutes while the yeast starts to get foamy.
2. Stir the melted butter, beaten egg, and vanilla extract into the bowl. Mix well until all of the ingredients are combined.
3. Fold in the plain flour and cocoa powder until a smooth mixture forms.
4. Lightly flour a clean kitchen top surface and roll the dough out. Gently knead the dough for 2-3 minutes until it becomes soft and slightly tacky.
5. Transfer the dough into a large mixing bowl and cover it with a clean tea towel or some tinfoil. Leave the dough to rise for around one hour in a warm place.

6. Remove the tea towel or tinfoil from the bowl and roll it out on a floured surface once again. Use a rolling pin to roll the dough into a one-inch thick circle.
7. Use a round cookie cutter to create circular donuts and place each one into a lined air fryer basket.
8. Once all of the donuts have been placed into the air fryer, turn the machine onto 150 ºC / 300 ºF and close the lid.
9. Cook the donuts for 8-10 minutes until they are slightly golden and crispy on the outside.
10. While the donuts are cooking in the air fryer, make the frosting by combining the powdered sugar, cocoa powder, heavy cream, and melted white chocolate chips in a bowl. Mix well until a smooth, sticky mixture forms.
11. When the donuts are cooked, remove them from the air fryer and set aside to cool for 5-10 minutes. Once cooled, evenly spread some frosting on the top layer of each one. Place in the fridge to set for at least one hour.
12. Enjoy the donuts hot or cold.

Sugar Dough Dippers

Servings: 12
Cooking Time:xx
Ingredients:
- 300g bread dough
- 75g melted butter
- 100g sugar
- 200ml double cream
- 200g semi sweet chocolate
- 2 tbsp amaretto

Directions:
1. Roll the dough into 2 15inch logs, cut each one into 20 slices. Cut each slice in half and twist together 2-3 times. Brush with melted butter and sprinkle with sugar
2. Preheat the air fryer to 150ºC
3. Place dough in the air fryer and cook for 5 minutes, turnover and cook for a further 3 minutes
4. Place the cream in a pan and bring to simmer over a medium heat, place the chocolate chips in a bowl and pour over the cream
5. Mix until the chocolate is melted then stir in the amaretto
6. Serve the dough dippers with the chocolate dip

Granola

Servings: 3
Cooking Time:xx
Ingredients:

- 60 g/¼ cup runny honey
- 50 g/3 tablespoons coconut oil
- 1 teaspoon vanilla extract
- 100 g/¾ cup jumbo rolled oats/old-fashioned oats (not porridge oats)
- 50 g/½ cup chopped walnuts
- 1 teaspoon ground cinnamon

Directions:

1. Preheat the air-fryer to 180ºC/350ºF.
2. Place the honey, coconut oil and vanilla extract in a small dish. Add this to the preheated air-fryer for 1 minute to melt.
3. In a small bowl combine the oats, nuts and cinnamon. Add the melted honey mixture and toss well, ensuring all the oats and nuts are well coated.
4. Lay an air-fryer liner or a pierced piece of parchment paper on the base of the air-fryer drawer. Add the granola mix on top, spread evenly in one layer. Air-fry for 4 minutes, then stir before cooking for a further 3 minutes. Leave to cool completely before serving or storing in a jar.

Brownies

Servings: 6
Cooking Time:xx
Ingredients:

- 25g melted butter
- 50g sugar
- 1 egg
- ½ tsp vanilla
- 25g flour
- 3 tbsp cocoa
- ⅛ tsp baking powder
- ⅛ tsp salt

Directions:

1. Preheat the air fryer to 165ºC
2. Add all the wet ingredients to a bowl and combine.
3. Add the dry ingredients and mix well
4. Place the batter into a prepared pan and cook in the air fryer for 13 minutes

Lava Cakes

Servings: 4
Cooking Time:xx
Ingredients:

- 1 ½ tbsp self raising flour
- 3 ½ tbsp sugar
- 150g butter
- 150g dark chocolate, chopped
- 2 eggs

Directions:

1. Preheat the air fryer to 175ºC
2. Grease 4 ramekin dishes
3. Melt chocolate and butter in the microwave for about 3 minutes
4. Whisk the eggs and sugar together until pale and frothy
5. Pour melted chocolate into the eggs and stir in the flour
6. Fill the ramekins ¾ full, place in the air fryer and cook for 10 minutes

Chocolate Mug Cake

Servings: 1
Cooking Time:xx
Ingredients:

- 30g self raising flour
- 5 tbsp sugar
- 1 tbsp cocoa powder
- 3 tbsp milk
- 3 tsp coconut oil

Directions:

1. Mix all the ingredients together in a mug
2. Heat the air fryer to 200ºC
3. Place the mug in the air fryer and cook for 10 minutes

Banana Cake

Servings: 4
Cooking Time:xx
Ingredients:

- Cooking spray
- 25g brown sugar
- ½ tbsp butter
- 1 banana, mashed
- 1 egg
- 2 tbsp honey
- 225g self raising flour
- ½ tsp cinnamon
- Pinch salt

Directions:

1. Preheat air fryer to 160°C
2. Spray a small fluted tube tray with cooking spray
3. Beat sugar and butter together in a bowl until creamy
4. Combine the banana egg and honey together in another bowl
5. Mix into the butter until smooth
6. Sift in the remaining ingredients and mix well
7. Spoon into the tray and cook in the air fryer for 30 minutes

Peanut Butter & Chocolate Baked Oats

Servings:9
Cooking Time:xx
Ingredients:

- 150 g/1 heaped cup rolled oats/quick-cooking oats
- 50 g/⅓ cup dark chocolate chips or buttons
- 300 ml/1¼ cups milk or plant-based milk
- 50 g/3½ tablespoons Greek or plant-based yogurt
- 1 tablespoon runny honey or maple syrup
- ½ teaspoon ground cinnamon or ground ginger
- 65 g/scant ⅓ cup smooth peanut butter

Directions:

1. Stir all the ingredients together in a bowl, then transfer to a baking dish that fits your air-fryer drawer.
2. Preheat the air-fryer to 180°C/350°F.

3. Add the baking dish to the preheated air-fryer and air-fry for 10 minutes. Remove from the air-fryer and serve hot, cut into 9 squares.

Profiteroles

Servings: 9
Cooking Time:xx
Ingredients:

- 100g butter
- 200g plain flour
- 6 eggs
- 300ml water
- 2 tsp vanilla extract
- 300ml whipped cream
- 100g milk chocolate
- 2 tbsp whipped cream
- 50g butter
- 2 tsp icing sugar

Directions:

1. Preheat the air fryer to 170°C
2. Place the butter and water in a pan over a medium heat, bring to the boil, remove from the heat and stir in the flour
3. Return to the heat stirring until a dough is formed
4. Mix in the eggs and stir until mixture is smooth, make into profiterole shapes and cook in the air fryer for 10 minutes
5. For the filling whisk together 300ml whipped cream, vanilla extract and the icing sugar
6. For the topping place the butter, 2tbsp whipped cream and chocolate in a bowl and melt over a pan of hot water until mixed together
7. Pipe the filling into the roles and finish off with a chocolate topping

Pecan & Molasses Flapjack

Servings:9
Cooking Time:xx
Ingredients:

- 120 g/½ cup plus 2 teaspoons butter or plant-based spread, plus extra for greasing
- 40 g/2 tablespoons blackstrap molasses
- 60 g/5 tablespoons unrefined sugar
- 50 g/½ cup chopped pecans
- 200 g/1½ cups porridge oats/steelcut oats (not rolled or jumbo)

Directions:

1. Preheat the air-fryer to 180°C/350°F.

2. Grease and line a 15 x 15-cm/6 x 6-in. baking pan.

3. In a large saucepan melt the butter/spread, molasses and sugar. Once melted, stir in the pecans, then the oats. As soon as they are combined, tip the mixture into the prepared baking pan and cover with foil.

4. Place the foil-covered baking pan in the preheated air-fryer and air-fry for 10 minutes. Remove the foil, then cook for a further 2 minutes to brown the top. Leave to cool, then cut into 9 squares.

Banana And Nutella Sandwich

Servings: 2
Cooking Time:xx
Ingredients:
- Softened butter
- 4 slices white bread
- 25g chocolate spread
- 1 banana

Directions:
1. Preheat the air fryer to 185°C
2. Spread butter on one side of all the bread slices
3. Spread chocolate spread on the other side of each slice
4. Add sliced banana to two slices of bread then add the other slice of bread to each
5. Cut in half diagonally to form triangles
6. Place in the air fryer and cook for 5 minutes turn over and cook for another 2 minutes

Chocolate And Berry Pop Tarts

Servings:8
Cooking Time:10 Minutes
Ingredients:
- For the filling:
- 50 g / 1.8 oz fresh raspberries
- 50 g / 1.8 oz fresh strawberries
- 100 g / 3.5 oz granulated sugar
- 1 tsp corn starch
- For the pastry:
- 1 sheet puff pastry
- For the frosting:
- 4 tbsp powdered sugar
- 2 tbsp maple syrup or honey
- Chocolate sprinkles

Directions:

1. Preheat the air fryer to 180 °C / 350 °F and line the mesh basket with parchment paper or grease it with olive oil.

2. Make the filling by combining the strawberries, raspberries, and granulated sugar in a saucepan. Place on medium heat until the mixture starts to boil. When it begins to boil, turn the temperature down to a low setting. Use a spoon to break up the berries and forms a smooth mixture.

3. Stir in the corn starch and let the mixture simmer for 1-2 minutes. Remove the saucepan from the heat and set aside to cool while you prepare the pastry.

4. Roll out the large sheet of puff pastry and cut it into 8 equal rectangles.

5. Spoon 2 tbsp of the cooled berry filling onto one side of each rectangle. Fold over the other side of each puff pastry rectangle to cover the filling. Press the sides down with a fork or using your fingers to seal the filling into the pastry.

6. Transfer the puff pastry rectangles into the lined air fryer basket. Cook for 10-12 minutes until the pastry is golden and crispy.

7. Meanwhile, make the frosting. Whisk together the powdered sugar, maple syrup or honey, and chocolate chips in a bowl until well combined.

8. Carefully spread a thin layer of frosting in the centre of each pop tart. Allow the frosting to set before serving.

Lemon Pies

Servings: 6
Cooking Time:xx
Ingredients:
- 1 pack of pastry
- 1 egg beaten
- 200g lemon curd
- 225g powdered sugar
- ½ lemon

Directions:
1. Preheat the air fryer to 180°C
2. Cut out 6 circles from the pastry using a cookie cutter
3. Add 1 tbsp of lemon curd to each circle, brush the edges with egg and fold over
4. Press around the edges of the dough with a fork to seal

5. Brush the pies with the egg and cook in the air fryer for 10 minutes
6. Mix the lemon juice with the powdered sugar to make the icing and drizzle on the cooked pies

Blueberry Muffins

Servings: 12
Cooking Time:xx
Ingredients:

- 500g cups self raising flour
- 50g monk fruit
- 50g cream
- 225g oil
- 2 eggs
- 200g blueberries
- Zest and juice of 1 lemon
- 1 tbsp vanilla

Directions:

1. Mix together flour and sugar, set aside
2. In another bowl mix the remaining ingredients
3. Mix in the flour
4. Spoon the mix into silicone cupcake cases
5. Place in the air fryer and cook at 160°C for about 10 minutes

Melting Moments

Servings: 9
Cooking Time:xx
Ingredients:

- 100g butter
- 75g caster sugar
- 150g self raising flour
- 1 egg
- 50g white chocolate
- 3 tbsp desiccated coconut
- 1 tsp vanilla essence

Directions:

1. Preheat the air fryer to 180°C
2. Cream together the butter and sugar, beat in the egg and vanilla
3. Bash the white chocolate into small pieces
4. Add the flour and chocolate and mix well
5. Roll into 9 small balls and cover in coconut
6. Place in the air fryer and cook for 8 minutes and a further 6 minutes at 160°C

Apple And Cinnamon Empanadas

Servings: 12
Cooking Time:xx
Ingredients:

- 12 empanada wraps
- 2 diced apples
- 2 tbsp honey
- 1 tsp vanilla extract
- 1 tsp cinnamon
- ⅛ tsp nutmeg
- Olive oil spray
- 2 tsp cornstarch
- 1 tsp water

Directions:

1. Place apples, cinnamon, honey, vanilla and nutmeg in a pan cook for 2-3 minutes until apples are soft
2. Mix the cornstarch and water add to the pan and cook for 30 seconds
3. Add the apple mix to each of the empanada wraps
4. Roll the wrap in half, pinch along the edges, fold the edges in then continue to roll to seal
5. Place in the air fryer and cook at 200°C for 8 minutes, turn and cook for another 10 minutes

Chocolate Eclairs

Servings: 9
Cooking Time:xx
Ingredients:

- 100g plain flour
- 50g butter
- 3 eggs
- 150ml water
- 25g butter
- 1 tsp vanilla extract
- 1 tsp icing sugar
- 150ml whipped cream
- 50g milk chocolate
- 1 tbsp whipped cream

Directions:

1. Preheat the air fryer to 180°C
2. Add 50g of butter to a pan along with the water and melt over a medium heat
3. Remove from the heat and stir in the flour. Return to the heat until mix form a single ball of dough

4. Allow to cool, once cool beat in the eggs until you have a smooth dough
5. Make into eclair shapes, cook in the air fryer at 180°C for 10 minutes and then 160°C for 8 minutes
6. Mix the vanilla, icing sugar and 150ml of whipping cream until nice and thick
7. Once cool fill each eclair with the cream mix
8. Place the chocolate, 1 tbsp whipped cream and 25g of butter in a glass bowl and melt over a pan of boiling water. Top the eclairs

Grain-free Millionaire's Shortbread

Servings:9
Cooking Time:xx
Ingredients:

- BASE
- 60 g/5 tablespoons coconut oil
- 1 tablespoon maple syrup
- ½ teaspoon vanilla extract
- 180 g/1¾ cups ground almonds
- a pinch of salt
- MIDDLE
- 185 g/1⅓ cups dried pitted dates (soak in hot water for at least 20 minutes, then drain)
- 2 tablespoons almond butter
- 90 g/scant ½ cup canned coconut milk (the thick part once it has separated is ideal)
- TOPPING
- 125 g/½ cup coconut oil
- 4 tablespoons cacao powder
- 1 tablespoon maple syrup

Directions:

1. Preheat the air-fryer to 180°C/350°F.
2. To make the base, in a small saucepan melt the coconut oil with the maple syrup and vanilla extract. As soon as the coconut oil is melted, stir in the almonds and the salt off the heat. Press this mixture into a 15 x 15-cm/6 x 6-in. baking pan.
3. Add the baking pan to the preheated air-fryer and cook for 4 minutes, until golden brown on top. Remove from the air-fryer and allow to cool.
4. In a food processor, combine the rehydrated drained dates, almond butter and coconut milk. Once the base is cool, pour this mixture over

the base and pop into the freezer to set for an hour.
5. After the base has had 45 minutes in the freezer, make the topping by heating the coconut oil in a saucepan until melted, then whisk in the cacao powder and maple syrup off the heat to make a chocolate syrup. Leave this to cool for 15 minutes, then pour over the set middle layer and return to the freezer for 30 minutes. Cut into 9 squares to serve.

Special Oreos

Servings: 9
Cooking Time:xx
Ingredients:

- 100g pancake mix
- 25ml water
- Cooking spray
- 9 Oreos
- 1 tbsp icing sugar

Directions:

1. Mix pancake mix and water until well combined
2. Line the air fryer with parchment paper and spray with cooking spray
3. Preheat the air fryer to 200°C
4. Dip each cookie in the pancake mix and place in the air fryer
5. Cook for 5 minutes, turn and cook for a further 3 minutes
6. Sprinkle with icing sugar to serve

French Toast Sticks

Servings: 12
Cooking Time:xx
Ingredients:

- 2 eggs
- 25g milk
- 1 tbsp melted butter
- 1 tsp vanilla extract
- 1 tsp cinnamon
- 4 slices bread, cut into thirds
- 1 tsp icing sugar

Directions:

1. Mix eggs, milk, butter, vanilla and cinnamon together in a bowl
2. Line the air fryer with parchment paper
3. Dip each piece of bread into the egg mixture

4. Place in the air fryer and cook at 190ºC for 6 minutes, turn over and cook for another 3 minutes
5. Sprinkle with icing sugar to serve

Peanut Butter And Banana Bites

Servings: 12
Cooking Time:xx
Ingredients:

- 1 banana
- 12 wonton wrappers
- 75g peanut butter
- 1-2 tsp vegetable oil

Directions:

1. Slice the banana and place in a bowl of water with lemon juice to prevent browning
2. Place one piece of banana and a spoon of peanut butter in each wonton wrapper
3. Wet the edges of each wrapper and fold over to seal
4. Spray the air fryer with oil
5. Place in the air fryer and cook at 190ºC for 6 minutes

Banana Bread

Servings: 8
Cooking Time:xx
Ingredients:

- 200g flour
- 1 tsp cinnamon
- ½ tsp salt
- ¼ tsp baking soda
- 2 ripe banana mashed
- 2 large eggs
- 75g sugar
- 25g plain yogurt
- 2 tbsp oil
- 1 tsp vanilla extract
- 2 tbsp chopped walnuts
- Cooking spray

Directions:

1. Line a 6 inch cake tin with parchment paper and coat with cooking spray
2. Whisk together flour, cinnamon, salt and baking soda set aside
3. In another bowl mix together remaining ingredients, add the flour mix and combine well

4. Pour batter into the cake tin and place in the air fryer
5. Cook at 155ºC for 35 minutes turning halfway through

Pop Tarts

Servings: 6
Cooking Time:xx
Ingredients:

- 200g strawberries quartered
- 25g sugar
- ½ pack ready made pie crust
- Cooking spray
- 50g powdered sugar
- 1 ½ tsp lemon juice
- 1 tbsp sprinkles

Directions:

1. Stir together strawberries and sugar in a bowl
2. Allow to stand for 15 minutes then microwave on high for 10 minutes stirring halfway through
3. Roll out pie crust into 12 inch circle, cut into 12 rectangles
4. Spoon mix onto 6 of the rectangles
5. Brush the edges with water and top with the remaining rectangles
6. Press around the edges with a fork to seal
7. Place in the air fryer and cook at 175ºC for about 10 minutes
8. Mix together powdered sugar and decorate add sprinkles

Chocolate-glazed Banana Slices

Servings:2
Cooking Time:10 Minutes
Ingredients:

- 2 bananas
- 1 tbsp honey
- 1 tbsp chocolate spread, melted
- 2 tbsp milk chocolate chips

Directions:

1. Preheat the air fryer to 180 ºC / 350 ºF. Remove the mesh basket from the machine and line it with parchment paper.
2. Cut the two bananas into even slices and place them in the lined air fryer basket.
3. In a small bowl, mix the honey and melted chocolate spread. Use a brush to glaze the banana slices. Carefully press the milk

97

chocolate chips into the banana slices enough so that they won't fall out when you transfer the bananas into the air fryer.

4. Carefully slide the mesh basket into the air fryer, close the lid, and cook for 10 minutes until the bananas are hot and the choc chips have melted.

5. Enjoy the banana slices on their own or with a side of ice cream.

Apple Chips With Yogurt Dip

Servings: 4
Cooking Time:xx
Ingredients:

- 1 apple
- 1 tsp cinnamon
- 2 tsp oil
- Cooking spray
- 25g greek yogurt
- 1 tbsp almond butter
- 1 tsp honey

Directions:

1. Thinly slice the apple, place in a bowl and coat with cinnamon and oil
2. Coat the air fryer with cooking spray and add the apple slices
3. Cook the slices for 12 minutes at 180ºC
4. Mix the butter, honey and yogurt together and serve with the apple slices as a dip

Banana Maple Flapjack

Servings:9
Cooking Time:xx
Ingredients:

- 100 g/7 tablespoons butter (or plant-based spread if you wish)
- 75 g/5 tablespoons maple syrup
- 2 ripe bananas, mashed well with the back of a fork
- 1 teaspoon vanilla extract
- 240 g/2½ cups rolled oats/quick-cooking oats

Directions:

1. Gently heat the butter and maple syrup in a medium saucepan over a low heat until melted. Stir in the mashed banana, vanilla and oats and combine all ingredients. Pour the flapjack mixture into a 15 x 15-cm/6 x 6-in. baking pan and cover with foil.
2. Preheat the air-fryer to 200ºC/400ºF.

3. Add the baking pan to the preheated air-fryer and air-fry for 12 minutes, then remove the foil and cook for a further 4 minutes to brown the top. Leave to cool before cutting into 9 squares.

Crispy Snack Apples

Servings: 2
Cooking Time:xx
Ingredients:

- 3 apples, Granny Smith work best
- 250g flour
- 3 whisked eggs
- 25g sugar
- 1 tsp ground cinnamon
- 250g cracker crumbs

Directions:

1. Preheat the air fryer to 220ºC
2. Peel the apples, remove the cores and cut into wedges
3. Take three bowls - the first with the flour, the second with the egg, and then this with the cracker crumbs, sugar and cinnamon combined
4. Dip the apple wedges into the egg in order
5. Place in the air fryer and cook for 5 minutes, turning over with one minute remaining

Cinnamon Biscuit Bites

Servings: 16
Cooking Time:xx
Ingredients:

- 200g flour
- 200g wholewheat flour
- 2 tbsp sugar
- 1 tsp baking powder
- ¼ tsp cinnamon
- ¼ tsp salt
- 4 tbsp butter
- 50ml milk
- Cooking spray
- 300g icing sugar
- 3 tbsp water

Directions:

1. Mix together flour, salt, sugar baking powder and cinnamon in a bowl
2. Add butter and mix until well combined
3. Add milk and form a dough, place dough on a floured surface and knead until smooth
4. Cut into 16 equal pieces and form each piece into a ball

5. Place in the air fryer and cook at 180ºC for about 12 minutes
6. Mix together icing sugar and water and coat to serve

Strawberry Lemonade Pop Tarts

Servings: 12
Cooking Time:xx
Ingredients:

- 300g whole wheat flour
- 225g white flour
- ¼ tsp salt
- 2 tbsp light brown sugar
- 300g icing sugar
- 2 tbsp lemon juice
- Zest of 1 lemon
- 150g cold coconut oil
- 1 tsp vanilla extract
- 75ml ice cold water
- Strawberry Jam
- 1 tsp melted coconut oil
- ¼ tsp vanilla extract
- Sprinkles

Directions:

1. In a bowl mix the flours, salt and sugar. Mix in the cold coconut oil
2. Add 1 tsp vanilla and 1 tbsp at a time of the ice cold water, mix until a dough is formed
3. Take the dough and roll out thinly on a floured surface. Cut into 5cm by 7cm rectangles
4. Place a tsp of jam in the centre of half the rectangles, wet the edges place another rectangle on the top and seal
5. Place in the air fryer and cook at 200ºC for 10 minutes. Allow to cool
6. Mix the icing sugar, coconut oil, lemon juice and lemon zest in a bowl. Mix well. Top the pop tarts and add sprinkles to serve

Cherry Pies

Servings: 6
Cooking Time:xx
Ingredients:

- 300g prepared shortcrust pastry
- 75g cherry pie filling
- Cooking spray
- 3 tbsp icing sugar
- ½ tsp milk

Directions:

1. Cut out 6 pies with a cookie cutter
2. Add 1 ½ tbsp filling to each pie
3. Fold the dough in half and seal around the edges with a fork
4. Place in the air fryer, spray with cooking spray
5. Cook at 175ºC for 10 minutes
6. Mix icing sugar and milk and drizzled over cooled pies to serve

Chocolate Shortbread Balls

Servings: 9
Cooking Time:13 Minutes
Ingredients:

- 175g butter
- 75g caster sugar
- 250g plain flour
- 2 tsp vanilla essence
- 9 chocolate chunks
- 2 tbsp cocoa powder

Directions:

1. Preheat the air fryer to 180ºC
2. Add the flour, sugar and cocoa to a bowl and mix well
3. Rub in the butter and vanilla then knead into a smooth dough
4. Divide the mix into 9, place a chunk of chocolate in each piece and form into balls covering the chocolate
5. Place the balls in the air fryer and cook at 180ºC for 8 mins then a further 6 mins at 160ºC

Thai Fried Bananas

Servings: 8
Cooking Time:xx
Ingredients:

- 4 ripe bananas
- 2 tbsp flour
- 2 tbsp rice flour
- 2 tbsp cornflour
- 2 tbsp desiccated coconut
- Pinch salt
- ½ tsp baking powder
- ½ tsp cardamon powder

Directions:

1. Place all the dry ingredients in a bowl and mix well. Add a little water at a time and combine to form a batter

2. Cut the bananas in half and then half again length wise
3. Line the air fryer with parchment paper and spray with cooking spray
4. Dip each banana piece in the batter mix and place in the air fryer
5. Cook at 200°C for 10 -15 minutes turning halfway
6. Serve with ice cream

Breakfast Muffins

Servings:4
Cooking Time:xx
Ingredients:

- 1 eating apple, cored and grated
- 40 g/2 heaped tablespoons maple syrup
- 40 ml/3 tablespoons oil (avocado, olive or coconut), plus extra for greasing
- 1 egg
- 40 ml/3 tablespoons milk (plant-based if you wish)
- 90 g/scant ¾ cup brown rice flour
- 50 g/½ cup ground almonds
- ¾ teaspoon ground cinnamon
- ⅛ teaspoon ground cloves
- ¼ teaspoon salt
- 1 teaspoon baking powder
- Greek or plant-based yogurt and fresh fruit, to serve

Directions:

1. In a bowl mix the grated apple, maple syrup, oil, egg and milk. In another bowl mix the rice flour, ground almonds, cinnamon, cloves, salt and baking powder. Combine the wet ingredients with the dry, mixing until there are no visible patches of the flour mixture left. Grease 4 ramekins and divide the batter equally between them.
2. Preheat the air-fryer to 160°C/325°F.
3. Add the ramekins to the preheated air-fryer and air-fry for 12 minutes. Check the muffins are cooked by inserting a cocktail stick/toothpick into the middle of one of the muffins. If it comes out clean, the muffins are ready; if not, cook for a further couple of minutes.
4. Allow to cool in the ramekins, then remove and serve with your choice of yogurt and fresh fruit.

Side Dishes Recipes

Sweet And Sticky Parsnips And Carrots

Servings:2
Cooking Time:15 Minutes
Ingredients:

- 4 large carrots, peeled and chopped into long chunks
- 4 large parsnips, peeled and chopped into long chunks
- 1 tbsp olive oil
- 2 tbsp honey
- 1 tsp dried mixed herbs

Directions:

1. Preheat the air fryer to 150 °C / 300 °F and line the bottom of the basket with parchment paper.
2. Place the chopped carrots and parsnips in a large bowl and drizzle over the olive oil and honey. Sprinkle in some black pepper to taste and toss well to fully coat the vegetables.
3. Transfer the coated vegetables into the air fryer basket and shut the lid. Cook for 20 minutes until the carrots and parsnips and cooked and crispy.
4. Serve as a side with your dinner.

Mediterranean Vegetables

Servings: 1–2
Cooking Time:xx
Ingredients:

- 1 courgette/zucchini, thickly sliced
- 1 (bell) pepper, deseeded and chopped into large chunks
- 1 red onion, sliced into wedges
- 12 cherry tomatoes
- 1 tablespoon olive oil
- ½ teaspoon salt
- ½ teaspoon freshly ground black pepper
- 2 rosemary twigs
- mozzarella, fresh pesto (see page 80) and basil leaves, to serve

Directions:

1. Preheat the air-fryer to 180°C/350°F.
2. Toss the prepared vegetables in the oil and seasoning. Add the vegetables and the rosemary to the preheated air-fryer and air-fry for 12–14 minutes, depending on how 'chargrilled' you like them.
3. Remove and serve topped with fresh mozzarella and pesto and scattered with basil leaves.

Potato Wedges

Servings: 4
Cooking Time:xx
Ingredients:

- 2 potatoes, cut into wedges
- 1 ½ tbsp olive oil
- ½ tsp paprika
- ⅛ tsp ground black pepper
- ½ tsp parsley flakes
- ½ tsp chilli powder
- ½ tsp sea salt

Directions:

1. Preheat the air fryer to 200°C
2. Add all ingredients to a bowl and combine well
3. Place the wedges into the air fryer and cook for 10 minutes
4. Turn and cook for a further 8 minutes until golden brown

Crispy Broccoli

Servings: 2
Cooking Time:xx
Ingredients:

- 170 g/6 oz. broccoli florets
- 2 tablespoons olive oil
- ⅛ teaspoon garlic salt
- ⅛ teaspoon freshly ground black pepper
- 2 tablespoons freshly grated Parmesan or Pecorino

Directions:

1. Preheat the air-fryer to 200°C/400°F.
2. Toss the broccoli in the oil, season with the garlic salt and pepper, then toss over the grated cheese and combine well. Add the broccoli to the preheated air-fryer and air-fry for 5 minutes, giving the broccoli a stir halfway through to ensure even cooking.

Zingy Roasted Carrots

Servings: 4
Cooking Time:xx
Ingredients:

- 500g carrots
- 1 tsp olive oil
- 1 tsp cayenne pepper
- Salt and pepper for seasoning

Directions:

1. Peel the carrots and cut them into chunks, around 2" in size
2. Preheat your air fryer to 220°C
3. Add the carrots to a bowl with the olive oil and cayenne and toss to coat
4. Place in the fryer and cook for 15 minutes, giving them a stir halfway through
5. Season before serving

Honey Roasted Parsnips

Servings: 4
Cooking Time:xx
Ingredients:

- 350 g/12 oz. parsnips
- 1 tablespoon plain/all-purpose flour (gluten-free if you wish)
- 1½ tablespoons runny honey
- 2 tablespoons olive oil
- salt

Directions:

1. Top and tail the parsnips, then slice lengthways, about 2 cm/¾ in. wide. Place in a saucepan with water to cover and a good pinch of salt. Bring to the boil, then boil for 5 minutes.
2. Remove and drain well, allowing any excess water to evaporate. Dust the parsnips with

flour. Mix together the honey and oil in a small bowl, then toss in the parsnips to coat well in the honey and oil.

3. Preheat the air-fryer to 180ºC/350ºF.
4. Add the parsnips to the preheated air-fryer and air-fry for 14–16 minutes, depending on how dark you like the outsides (the longer you cook them, the sweeter they get).

Crispy Cinnamon French Toast

Servings:2
Cooking Time:5 Minutes
Ingredients:

- 4 slices white bread
- 4 eggs
- 200 ml milk (cow's milk, cashew milk, soy milk, or oat milk)
- 2 tbsp granulated sugar
- 1 tsp brown sugar
- 1 tsp vanilla extract
- ½ tsp ground cinnamon

Directions:

1. Preheat your air fryer to 150 ºC / 300 ºF and line the bottom of the basket with parchment paper.
2. Cut each of the bread slices into 2 even rectangles and set them aside.
3. In a mixing bowl, whisk together the 4 eggs, milk, granulated sugar, brown sugar, vanilla extract, and ground cinnamon.
4. Soak the bread pieces in the egg mixture until they are fully covered and soaked in the mixture.
5. Place the coated bread slices in the lined air fryer, close the lid, and cook for 4-5 minutes until the bread is crispy and golden.
6. Serve the French toast slices with whatever toppings you desire.

Aubergine Parmesan

Servings: 4
Cooking Time:xx
Ingredients:

- 100g Italian breadcrumbs
- 50g grated parmesan
- 1 tsp Italian seasoning
- 1 tsp salt
- ½ tsp dried basil
- ½ tsp onion powder
- ½ tsp black pepper
- 100g flour
- 2 eggs
- 1 aubergine, sliced into ½ inch rounds

Directions:

1. Mix breadcrumbs, parmesan, salt Italian seasoning, basil, onion powder and pepper in a bowl
2. Add the flour to another bowl, and beat the eggs in another
3. Dip the aubergine in the flour, then the eggs and then coat in the bread crumbs
4. Preheat the air fryer to 185ºC
5. Place the aubergine in the air fryer and cook for 8-10 minutes
6. Turnover and cook for a further 4-6 minutes

Celery Root Fries

Servings: 2
Cooking Time:xx
Ingredients:

- ½ celeriac, cut into sticks
- 500ml water
- 1 tbsp lime juice
- 1 tbsp olive oil
- 75g mayo
- 1 tbsp mustard
- 1 tbsp powdered horseradish

Directions:

1. Put celeriac in a bowl, add water and lime juice, soak for 30 minutes
2. Preheat air fryer to 200
3. Mix together the mayo, horseradish powder and mustard, refrigerate
4. Drain the celeriac, drizzle with oil and season with salt and pepper
5. Place in the air fryer and cook for about 10 minutes turning halfway
6. Serve with the mayo mix as a dip

Onion Rings

Servings: 4
Cooking Time:xx
Ingredients:

- 200g flour
- 75g cornstarch
- 2 tsp baking powder
- 1 tsp salt
- 2 pinches of paprika
- 1 large onion, cut into rings

- 1 egg
- 1 cup milk
- 200g breadcrumbs
- 2 pinches garlic powder

Directions:
1. Stir flour, salt, starch and baking powder together in a bowl
2. Dip onion rings into the flour mix to coat
3. Whisk the egg and milk into the flour mix, dip in the onion rings
4. Dip the onion rings into the bread crumbs
5. Heat the air fryer to 200°C
6. Place the onion rings in the air fryer and cook for 2-3 minutes until golden brown
7. Sprinkle with paprika and garlic powder to serve

Cauliflower With Hot Sauce And Blue Cheese Sauce

Servings:2
Cooking Time:15 Minutes
Ingredients:
- For the cauliflower:
- 1 cauliflower, broken into florets
- 4 tbsp hot sauce
- 2 tbsp olive oil
- 1 tsp garlic powder
- ½ tsp salt
- ½ tsp black pepper
- 1 tbsp plain flour
- 1 tbsp corn starch
- For the blue cheese sauce:
- 50 g / 1.8 oz blue cheese, crumbled
- 2 tbsp sour cream
- 2 tbsp mayonnaise
- ½ tsp salt
- ½ tsp black pepper

Directions:
1. Preheat the air fryer to 180 °C / 350 °F and line the bottom of the basket with parchment paper.
2. In a bowl, combine the hot sauce, olive oil, garlic powder, salt, and black pepper until it forms a consistent mixture. Add the cauliflower to the bowl and coat in the sauce.
3. Stir in the plain flour and corn starch until well combined.
4. Transfer the cauliflower to the lined basket in the air fryer, close the lid, and cook for 12-15

minutes until the cauliflower has softened and is golden in colour.
5. Meanwhile, make the blue cheese sauce by combining all of the ingredients. When the cauliflower is ready, remove it from the air fryer and serve with the blue cheese sauce on the side.

Roasted Okra

Servings: 1
Cooking Time:xx
Ingredients:
- 300g Okra, ends trimmed and pods sliced
- 1 tsp olive oil
- ¼ tsp salt
- ⅛ tsp pepper

Directions:
1. Preheat the air fryer to 175°C
2. Combine all ingredients in a bowl and stir gently
3. Place in the air fryer and cook for 5 minutes, shake and cook for another 5 minutes

Garlic And Parsley Potatoes

Servings: 4
Cooking Time:xx
Ingredients:
- 500g baby potatoes, cut into quarters
- 1 tbsp oil
- 1 tsp salt
- ½ tsp garlic powder
- ½ tsp dried parsley

Directions:
1. Preheat air fryer to 175°C
2. Combine potatoes and oil in a bowl
3. Add remaining ingredients and mix
4. Add to the air fryer and cook for about 25 minutes until golden brown, turning halfway through

Air Fryer Eggy Bread

Servings:2
Cooking Time:5-7 Minutes
Ingredients:

- 4 slices white bread
- 4 eggs, beaten
- 1 tsp black pepper
- 1 tsp dried chives

Directions:

1. Preheat your air fryer to 150 °C / 300 °F and line the bottom of the basket with parchment paper.
2. Whisk the eggs in a large mixing bowl and soak each slice of bread until fully coated.
3. Transfer the eggy bread to the preheated air fryer and cook for 5-7 minutes until the eggs are set and the bread is crispy.
4. Serve hot with a sprinkle of black pepper and chives on top.

Asparagus Fries

Servings: 2
Cooking Time:xx
Ingredients:

- 1 egg
- 1 tsp honey
- 100g panko bread crumbs
- Pinch of cayenne pepper
- 100g grated parmesan
- 12 asparagus spears
- 75g mustard
- 75g Greek yogurt

Directions:

1. Preheat air fryer to 200ºC
2. Combine egg and honey in a bowl, mix panko crumbs and parmesan on a plate
3. Coat each asparagus in egg then in the bread crumbs
4. Place in the air fryer and cook for about 6 mins
5. Mix the remaining ingredients in a bowl and serve as a dipping sauce

Tex Mex Hash Browns

Servings: 4
Cooking Time:xx
Ingredients:

- 500g potatoes cut into cubes
- 1 tbsp olive oil
- 1 red pepper

- 1 onion
- 1 jalapeño pepper
- ½ tsp taco seasoning
- ½ tsp cumin
- Salt and pepper to taste

Directions:

1. Soak the potatoes in water for 20 minutes
2. Heat the air fryer to 160ºC
3. Drain the potatoes and coat with olive oil
4. Add to the air fryer and cook for 18 minutes
5. Mix the remaining ingredients in a bowl, add the potatoes and mix well
6. Place the mix into the air fryer cook for 6 minutes, shake and cook for a further 5 minutes

Pumpkin Fries

Servings: 4
Cooking Time:xx
Ingredients:

- 1 small pumpkin, seeds removed and peeled, cut into half inch slices
- 2 tsp olive oil
- 1 tsp garlic powder
- 1/2 tsp paprika
- A pinch of salt

Directions:

1. Take a large bowl and add the slices of pumpkin
2. Add the oil and all the seasonings. Toss to coat well
3. Place in the air fryer
4. Cook at 280ºC for 15 minutes, until the chips are tender, shaking at the halfway point

Ricotta Stuffed Aubergine

Servings: 2
Cooking Time:xx
Ingredients:

- 1 aubergine
- 150g ricotta cheese
- 75g Parmesan cheese, plus an extra 75g for the breading
- 1 tsp garlic powder
- 3 tbsp parsley
- 1 egg, plus an extra 2 eggs for the breading
- 300g pork rind crumbs
- 2 tsp Italian seasoning

Directions:

1. Cut the aubergine into rounds, about 1/2" in thickness
2. Line a baking sheet with parchment and arrange the rounds on top, sprinkling with salt
3. Place another sheet of parchment on top and place something heavy on top to get rid of excess water
4. Leave for 30 minutes
5. Take a bowl and combine the egg, ricotta, 75g Parmesan and parsley, until smooth
6. Remove the parchment from the aubergine and wipe off the salt
7. Take a tablespoon of the ricotta mixture and place on top of each round of aubergine, spreading with a knife
8. Place in the freezer for a while to set
9. Take a bowl and add the two eggs, the pork rinds, parmesan and seasonings, and combine
10. Remove the aubergine from the freezer and coat each one in the mixture completely
11. Place back in the freezer for 45 minutes
12. Cook in the air fryer for 8 minutes at 250°C

Corn On The Cob

Servings: 4
Cooking Time:xx
Ingredients:
- 75g mayo
- 2 tsp grated cheese
- 1 tsp lime juice
- ¼ tsp chilli powder
- 2 ears of corn, cut into 4

Directions:
1. Heat the air fryer to 200°C
2. Mix the mayo, cheese lime juice and chilli powder in a bowl
3. Cover the corn in the mayo mix
4. Place in the air fryer and cook for 8 minutes

Carrot & Parmesan Chips

Servings: 2
Cooking Time:xx
Ingredients:
- 180g carrots
- 1 tbsp olive oil
- 2 tbsp grated parmesan
- 1 crushed garlic clove
- Salt and pepper for seasoning

Directions:

1. Take a mixing bowl and add the olive oil and garlic, combining well
2. Remove the tops of the carrots and cut into halves, and then another half
3. Add the carrots to the bowl and toss well
4. Add the parmesan and coat the carrots well
5. Add the carrots to the air fryer and cook for 20 minutes at 220°C, shaking halfway through

Courgette Gratin

Servings: 2
Cooking Time:xx
Ingredients:
- 2 courgette
- 1 tbsp chopped parsley
- 2 tbsp breadcrumbs
- 4 tbsp grated parmesan
- 1 tbsp vegetable oil
- Salt and pepper to taste

Directions:
1. Heat the air fryer to 180°C
2. Cut each courgette in half length ways then slice
3. Mix the remaining ingredients together
4. Place the courgette in the air fryer and top with the breadcrumb mix
5. Cook for about 15 minutes until golden brown

Butternut Squash

Servings: 4
Cooking Time:xx
Ingredients:
- 500 g/1 lb. 2 oz. butternut squash, chopped into 2.5-cm/1-in. cubes
- 1 tablespoon olive oil or avocado oil
- 1 teaspoon smoked paprika
- 1 teaspoon dried oregano
- ½ teaspoon salt
- ¼ teaspoon freshly ground black pepper

Directions:
1. Preheat the air-fryer to 180°C/350°F.
2. In a bowl toss the butternut squash cubes in the oil and all the seasonings.
3. Add the butternut squash cubes to the preheated air-fryer and air-fry for 16–18 minutes, shaking the drawer once during cooking.

Orange Tofu

Servings: 4
Cooking Time:xx
Ingredients:

- 400g tofu, drained
- 1 tbsp tamari
- 1 tbsp corn starch
- ¼ tsp pepper flakes
- 1 tsp minced ginger
- 1 tsp fresh garlic
- 1 tsp orange zest
- 75ml orange juice
- 75ml water
- 2 tsp cornstarch
- 1 tbsp maple syrup

Directions:

1. Cut the tofu into cubes, place in a bowl add the tamari and mix well
2. Mix in 1 tbsp starch and allow to marinate for 30 minutes
3. Place the remaining ingredients into another bowl and mix well
4. Place the tofu in the air fryer and cook at 190°C for about 10 minutes
5. Add tofu to a pan with sauce mix and cook until sauce thickens

Orange Sesame Cauliflower

Servings: 4
Cooking Time:xx
Ingredients:

- 100ml water
- 30g cornstarch
- 50g flour
- 1/2 tsp salt
- ½ tsp pepper
- 2 tbsp tomato ketchup
- 2 tbsp brown sugar
- 1 sliced onion

Directions:

1. Mix together flour, cornstarch, water, salt and pepper until smooth
2. Coat the cauliflower and chill for 30 minutes
3. Place in the air fryer and cook for 22 minutes at 170°C
4. Meanwhile combine remaining ingredients in a saucepan, gently simmer until thickened.

5. Mix cauliflower with sauce and top with toasted sesame seeds to serve

Yorkshire Puddings

Servings: 2
Cooking Time:xx
Ingredients:

- 1 tablespoon olive oil
- 70 g/½ cup plus ½ tablespoon plain/all-purpose flour (gluten-free if you wish)
- 100 ml/7 tablespoons milk
- 2 eggs
- salt and freshly ground black pepper

Directions:

1. You will need 4 ramekins. Preheat the air-fryer to 200°C/400°F.
2. Using a pastry brush, oil the base and sides of each ramekin, dividing the oil equally between the ramekins. Place the greased ramekins in the preheated air-fryer and heat for 5 minutes.
3. Meanwhile, in a food processor or using a whisk, combine the flour, milk, eggs and seasoning until you have a batter that is frothy on top. Divide the batter equally between the preheated ramekins. Return the ramekins to the air-fryer and air-fry for 20 minutes without opening the drawer. Remove the Yorkshire puddings from the ramekins and serve immediately.

Egg Fried Rice

Servings:2
Cooking Time:15 Minutes
Ingredients:

- 400 g / 14 oz cooked white or brown rice
- 100 g / 3.5 oz fresh peas and sweetcorn
- 2 tbsp olive oil
- 2 eggs, scrambled

Directions:

1. Preheat the air fryer to 150 °C / 300 °F and line the bottom of the basket with parchment paper.
2. In a bowl, mix the cooked white or brown rice and the fresh peas and sweetcorn.
3. Pour in 2 tbsp olive oil and toss to coat evenly. Stir in the scrambled eggs.
4. Transfer the egg rice into the lined air fryer basket, close the lid, and cook for 15 minutes until the eggs are cooked and the rice is soft.
5. Serve as a side dish with some cooked meat or tofu.

Crispy Sweet & Spicy Cauliflower

Servings: 2
Cooking Time:xx
Ingredients:

- ½ a head of cauliflower
- 1 teaspoon sriracha sauce
- 1 teaspoon soy sauce (or tamari)
- ½ teaspoon maple syrup
- 2 teaspoons olive oil or avocado oil

Directions:

1. Preheat the air-fryer to 180°C/350°F.
2. Chop the cauliflower into florets with a head size of roughly 5 cm/1 in. Place the other ingredients in a bowl and mix together, then add the florets and toss to coat them.
3. Add the cauliflower to the preheated air-fryer and air-fry for 12 minutes, shaking the drawer a couple of times during cooking.

Spicy Green Beans

Servings: 4
Cooking Time:xx
Ingredients:

- 300g green beans
- 1 tbsp sesame oil
- 1 tsp soy
- 1 tsp rice wine vinegar
- 1 clove garlic, minced
- 1 tsp red pepper flakes

Directions:

1. Preheat air fryer to 200°C
2. Place green beans in a bowl
3. Mix together remaining ingredients, add green beans and fully coat
4. Place in the air fryer and cook for 12 minutes

Stuffing Filled Pumpkin

Servings: 2
Cooking Time:xx
Ingredients:

- 1/2 small pumpkin
- 1 diced parsnip
- 1 sweet potato, diced
- 1 diced onion
- 2 tsp dried mixed herbs
- 50g peas
- 1 carrot, diced
- 1 egg
- 2 minced garlic cloves

Directions:

1. Remove the seeds from the pumpkin
2. Combine all the other ingredients in a bowl
3. Stuff the pumpkin
4. Preheat the air fryer to 175°C
5. Place the pumpkin in the air fryer and cook for about 30 minutes

Sweet Potato Tots

Servings: 24
Cooking Time:xx
Ingredients:

- 2 sweet potatoes, peeled
- ½ tsp cajun seasoning
- Olive oil cooking spray
- Sea salt to taste

Directions:

1. Boil the sweet potatoes in a pan for about 15 minutes, allow to cool
2. Grate the sweet potato and mix in the cajun seasoning
3. Form into tot shaped cylinders
4. Spray the air fryer with oil, place the tots in the air fryer
5. Sprinkle with salt and cook for 8 minutes at 200°C, turn and cook for another 8 minutes

Sweet Potato Wedges

Servings:4
Cooking Time:20 Minutes
Ingredients:

- ½ tsp garlic powder
- ½ tsp cumin
- ½ tsp smoked paprika
- ½ tsp cayenne pepper
- ½ tsp salt
- ½ tsp black pepper
- 1 tsp dried chives
- 4 tbsp olive oil
- 3 large sweet potatoes, cut into wedges

Directions:

1. Preheat the air fryer to 180 °C / 350 °F and line the bottom of the basket with parchment paper.
2. In a bowl, mix the garlic powder, cumin, smoked paprika, cayenne pepper, salt, black pepper, and dried chives until combined.

3. Whisk in the olive oil and coat the sweet potato wedges in the spicy oil mixture.
4. Transfer the coated sweet potatoes to the air fryer and close the lid. Cook for 20 minutes until cooked and crispy. Serve hot as a side with your main meal.

Cheesy Garlic Asparagus

Servings: 4
Cooking Time:xx
Ingredients:
- 1 tsp olive oil
- 500g asparagus
- 1 tsp garlic salt
- 1 tbsp grated parmesan cheese
- Salt and pepper for seasoning

Directions:
1. Preheat the air fryer to 270°C
2. Clean the asparagus and cut off the bottom 1"
3. Pat dry and place in the air fryer, covering with the oil
4. Sprinkle the parmesan and garlic salt on top, seasoning to your liking
5. Cook for between 7 and 10 minutes
6. Add a little extra parmesan over the top before serving

Sweet & Spicy Baby Peppers

Servings: 2
Cooking Time:xx
Ingredients:
- 200 g/7 oz. piccarella (baby) peppers, deseeded and quartered lengthways
- 1 teaspoon olive oil
- ½ teaspoon chilli/chili paste
- ¼ teaspoon runny honey
- salt and freshly ground black pepper

Directions:
1. Preheat the air-fryer to 180°C/350°F.
2. Toss the peppers in the oil, chilli/chili paste and honey, then add salt and pepper to taste.
3. Place in the preheated air-fryer and air-fry for 6–8 minutes, depending on how 'chargrilled' you like them, turning them over halfway through.

Asparagus Spears

Servings: 2
Cooking Time:xx
Ingredients:

- 1 bunch of trimmed asparagus
- 1 teaspoon olive oil
- ¼ teaspoon salt
- ⅛ teaspoon freshly ground black pepper

Directions:
1. Preheat the air-fryer to 180°C/350°F.
2. Toss the asparagus spears in the oil and seasoning. Add these to the preheated air-fryer and air-fry for 8–12 minutes, turning once (cooking time depends on the thickness of the stalks, which should retain some bite).

Air Fryer Corn On The Cob

Servings: 2
Cooking Time:xx
Ingredients:
- 2 corn on the cob
- 2 tbsp melted butter
- A pinch of salt
- 1/2 tsp dried parsley
- 2 tbsp grated parmesan

Directions:
1. Preheat the air fryer to 270°C
2. Take a bowl and combine the melted butter, salt and parsley
3. Brush the corn with the mixture
4. Add the corn inside the air fryer and cook for 14 minutes
5. Remove the corn from the fryer and roll in the grated cheese

Cheesy Broccoli

Servings:4
Cooking Time:5 Minutes
Ingredients:
- 1 large broccoli head, broken into florets
- 4 tbsp soft cheese
- 1 tsp black pepper
- 50 g / 3.5 oz cheddar cheese, grated

Directions:
1. Preheat the air fryer to 150 °C / 300 °F and line the mesh basket with parchment paper or grease it with olive oil.
2. Wash and drain the broccoli florets and place in a bowl and stir in the soft cheese and black pepper to fully coat all of the florets.
3. Transfer the broccoli to the air fryer basket and sprinkle the cheddar cheese on top. Close the lid and cook for 5-7 minutes until the broccoli has softened and the cheese has melted.

4. Serve as a side dish to your favourite meal.

Stuffed Jacket Potatoes

Servings: 4
Cooking Time:xx
Ingredients:
- 2 large russet potatoes
- 2 tsp olive oil
- 100ml yoghurt
- 100ml milk
- ¼ tsp pepper
- 50g chopped spinach
- 2 tbsp nutritional yeast
- ½ tsp salt

Directions:
1. Preheat the air fryer to 190°C
2. Rub the potatoes with oil
3. Place the potatoes in the air fryer and cook for 30 minutes, turn and cook for a further 30 minutes
4. Cut each potato in half and scoop out the middles, mash with yoghurt, milk and yeast. Stir in the spinach and season with salt and pepper
5. Add the mix back into the potato skins and place in the air fryer, cook at 160°C for about 5 mins

Potato Wedges With Rosemary

Servings: 2
Cooking Time:xx
Ingredients:
- 2 potatoes, sliced into wedges
- 1 tbsp olive oil
- 2 tsp seasoned salt
- 2 tbsp chopped rosemary

Directions:
1. Preheat air fryer to 190°C
2. Drizzle potatoes with oil, mix in salt and rosemary
3. Place in the air fryer and cook for 20 minutes turning halfway

Potato Hay

Servings: 4
Cooking Time:xx
Ingredients:
- 2 potatoes
- 1 tbsp oil

- Salt and pepper to taste

Directions:
1. Cut the potatoes into spirals
2. Soak in a bowl of water for 20 minutes, drain and pat dry
3. Add oil, salt and pepper and mix well to coat
4. Preheat air fryer to 180°C
5. Add potatoes to air fryer and cook for 5 minutes, toss then cook for another 12 until golden brown

Homemade Croquettes

Servings:4
Cooking Time:15 Minutes
Ingredients:
- 400 g / 14 oz white rice, uncooked
- 1 onion, sliced
- 2 cloves garlic, finely sliced
- 2 eggs, beaten
- 50 g / 3.5 oz parmesan cheese, grated
- 1 tsp salt
- 1 tsp black pepper
- 50 g / 3.5 oz breadcrumbs
- 1 tsp dried oregano

Directions:
1. In a large mixing bowl, combine the white rice, onion slices, garlic cloves slices, one beaten egg, parmesan cheese, and a sprinkle of salt and pepper.
2. Whisk the second egg in a separate bowl and place the breadcrumbs into another bowl.
3. Shape the mixture into 12 even croquettes and roll evenly in the egg, followed by the breadcrumbs.
4. Preheat the air fryer to 190 °C / 375 °F and line the bottom of the basket with parchment paper.
5. Place the croquettes in the lined air fryer basket and cook for 15 minutes, turning halfway through, until crispy and golden. Enjoy while hot as a side to your main dish.

Mexican Rice

Servings: 4
Cooking Time:xx
Ingredients:
- 500g long grain rice
- 3 tbsp olive oil
- 60ml water
- 1 tsp chilli powder

- 1/4 tsp cumin
- 2 tbsp tomato paste
- 1/2 tsp garlic powder
- 1tsp red pepper flakes
- 1 chopped onion
- 500ml chicken stock
- Half a small jalapeño pepper with seeds out, chopped
- Salt for seasoning

Directions:

1. Add the water and tomato paste and combine, placing to one side
2. Take a baking pan and add a little oil
3. Wash the rice and add to the baking pan
4. Add the chicken stock, tomato paste, jalapeños, onions, and the rest of the olive oil, and combine
5. Place aluminium foil over the top and place in your air fryer
6. Cook at 220°C for 50 minutes
7. Keep checking the rice as it cooks, as the liquid should be absorbing

Alternative Stuffed Potatoes

Servings: 4
Cooking Time:xx
Ingredients:

- 4 baking potatoes, peeled and halved
- 1 tbsp olive oil
- 150g grated cheese
- ½ onion, diced
- 2 slices bacon

Directions:

1. Preheat air fryer to 175°C
2. Brush the potatoes with oil and cook in the air fryer for 10 minutes
3. Coat again with oil and cook for a further 10 minutes
4. Cut the potatoes in half spoon the insides into a bowl and mix in the cheese
5. Place the bacon and onion in a pan and cook until browned, mix in with the potato
6. Stuff the skins with the mix and return to the air fryer, cook for about 6 minutes

Whole Sweet Potatoes

Servings: 4 As A Side Or Snack
Cooking Time:xx
Ingredients:

- 4 medium sweet potatoes
- 1 tablespoon olive oil
- 1 teaspoon salt
- toppings of your choice

Directions:

1. Preheat the air-fryer to 200°C/400°F.
2. Wash and remove any imperfections from the skin of the sweet potatoes, then rub the potatoes with the olive oil and salt.
3. Add the sweet potatoes to the preheated air-fryer and air-fry for up to 40 minutes (the cooking time depends on the size of the potatoes). Remove as soon as they are soft when pierced. Slice open and serve with your choice of toppings.
4. VARIATION: WHOLE JACKET POTATOES
5. Regular baking potatoes can be air-fried in the same way, but will require a cooking time of 45–60 minutes, depending on their size.

Shishito Peppers

Servings: 2
Cooking Time:xx
Ingredients:

- 200g shishito peppers
- Salt and pepper to taste
- ½ tbsp avocado oil
- 75g grated cheese
- 2 limes

Directions:

1. Rinse the peppers
2. Place in a bowl and mix with oil, salt and pepper
3. Place in the air fryer and cook at 175°C for 10 minutes
4. Place on a serving plate and sprinkle with cheese

Bbq Beetroot Crisps

Servings:4
Cooking Time:5 Minutes
Ingredients:

- 400 g / 14 oz beetroot, sliced
- 2 tbsp olive oil
- 1 tbsp BBQ seasoning
- ½ tsp black pepper

Directions:

1. Preheat the air fryer to 180 °C / 350 °F and line the bottom of the basket with parchment paper.

2. Place the beetroot slices in a large bowl. Add the olive oil, BBQ seasoning, and black pepper, and toss to coat the beetroot slices on both sides.
3. Place the beetroot slices in the air fryer and cook for 5 minutes until hot and crispy.

Ranch-style Potatoes

Servings: 2
Cooking Time:xx
Ingredients:
- 300g baby potatoes, washed
- 1 tbsp olive oil
- 3 tbsp dry ranch seasoning

Directions:
1. Preheat the air fryer to 220°C
2. Cut the potatoes in half
3. Take a mixing bowl and combine the olive oil with the ranch seasoning
4. Add the potatoes to the bowl and toss to coat
5. Cook for 15 minutes, shaking halfway through

Roasted Brussels Sprouts

Servings: 3
Cooking Time:xx
Ingredients:
- 300 g/10½ oz. Brussels sprouts, trimmed and halved
- 1 tablespoon olive oil
- ½ teaspoon salt
- ¼ teaspoon freshly ground black pepper

Directions:
1. Preheat the air-fryer to 160°C/325°F.
2. Toss the Brussels sprout halves in the oil and the seasoning. Add these to the preheated air-fryer and air-fry for 15 minutes, then increase the temperature of the air-fryer to 180°C/350°F and cook for a further 5 minutes until the sprouts are really crispy on the outside and cooked through.

Hasselback New Potatoes

Servings: 4
Cooking Time:xx
Ingredients:
- 8–12 new potatoes, roughly 5–7 cm/2–2¾ in. in length
- 2 teaspoons olive oil
- salt

- 1 tablespoon butter (optional)

Directions:
1. Preheat the air-fryer to 180°C/350°F.
2. Slice the potatoes multiple times widthways, making sure you do not cut all the way through (if you place the potatoes in the bowl of a wooden spoon to make these slices, it prevents you cutting all the way through). Coat the potatoes in the olive oil and sprinkle over the salt.
3. Add the potatoes to the preheated air-fryer and air-fry for 20–25 minutes until the potatoes are crispy on the outside but soft on the inside. Serve immediately.

Butternut Squash Fries

Servings: 4
Cooking Time:xx
Ingredients:
- 400g butternut squash, cut into sticks
- 1 tbsp olive oil
- 2 tbsp bagel seasoning
- 1 tsp fresh chopped rosemary

Directions:
1. Preheat air fryer to 200°C
2. Drizzle butternut squash with olive oil mix to coat
3. Add to the air fryer, cook for about 22 minutes until golden brown, stirring every 4 minutes
4. Sprinkle with bagel seasoning to serve

Zingy Brussels Sprouts

Servings: 2
Cooking Time:xx
Ingredients:
- 1 tbsp avocado oil
- ½ tsp salt
- ½ tsp pepper
- 400g Brussels sprouts halved
- 1 tsp balsamic vinegar
- 2 tsp crumbled bacon

Directions:
1. Preheat air fryer to 175°C
2. Combine oil, salt and pepper in a bowl and mix well. Add Brussels sprouts
3. Place in the air fryer and cook for 5 minutes shake then cook for another 5 minutes
4. Sprinkle with balsamic vinegar and sprinkle with bacon

RECIPES INDEX

Cheese Wontons 70
Cheese, Tomato & Pesto Crustless Quiches 79
Cheesy Beef Enchiladas 41
Cheesy Broccoli 108
Cheesy Garlic Asparagus 108
Cheesy Meatball Sub 36
Cheesy Sausage Breakfast Pockets 17
Cheesy Taco Crescents 64
Cherry Pies 99
Chicken & Bacon Parcels 69
Chicken & Potatoes 48
Chicken And Cheese Chimichangas 48
Chicken And Wheat Stir Fry 51
Chicken Balls, Greek-style 58
Chicken Fajitas 52
Chicken Fried Rice 56
Chicken Jalfrezi 59
Chicken Kiev 56
Chicken Milanese 60
Chicken Parmesan With Marinara Sauce 53
Chicken Tikka 59
Chicken Tikka Masala 53
Chickpea And Sweetcorn Falafel 83
Chickpea Falafel 80
Chilli Lime Tilapia 27
Chinese Chilli Beef 38
Chinese Pork With Pineapple 35
Chocolate And Berry Pop Tarts 94
Chocolate Cake 89
Chocolate Eclairs 95
Chocolate Mug Cake 92
Chocolate Shortbread Balls 99
Chocolate Souffle 89
Chocolate-glazed Banana Slices 97
Chonut Holes 89
Christmas Biscuits 90
Cinnamon Biscuit Bites 98
Cinnamon-maple Pineapple Kebabs 87
Coconut Shrimp 22
Cod In Parma Ham 26
Cod Nuggets 30
Copycat Fish Fingers 24
Corn Nuts 70
Corn On The Cob 105
Cornflake Chicken Nuggets 53
Courgette Burgers 83
Courgette Fries 14

Courgette Gratin 105
Courgette Meatballs 78
Crispy Broccoli 101
Crispy Cajun Fish Fingers 33
Crispy Chili Sausages 44
Crispy Cinnamon French Toast 102
Crispy Cornish Hen 56
Crispy Nacho Prawns 34
Crispy Potato Peels 80
Crispy Snack Apples 98
Crispy Sweet & Spicy Cauliflower 107
Crunchy Chicken Tenders 55
Crunchy Fish 34
Crunchy Mexican Breakfast Wrap 19
Cumin Shoestring Carrots 20

D
Delicious Breakfast Casserole 13
E
Easy Air Fryer Sausage 22
Easy Cheese & Bacon Toasties 18
Easy Cheesy Scrambled Eggs 11
Easy Omelette 12
Egg & Bacon Breakfast Cups 15
Egg Fried Rice 106
European Pancakes 10
Extra Crispy Popcorn Shrimp 29
F
Fillet Mignon Wrapped In Bacon 36
Fish In Foil 24
Fish In Parchment Paper 26
Fish Sticks With Tartar Sauce Batter 23
Fish Taco Cauliflower Rice Bowls 32
Flat Mushroom Pizzas 76
Focaccia Bread 72
French Toast 15
French Toast Slices 10
French Toast Sticks 96
Fruit Crumble 87
Furikake Salmon 30
G
Garlic And Parsley Potatoes 103
Garlic Butter Salmon 23
Garlic Cheese Bread 62
Garlic Parmesan Fried Chicken Wings 57
Garlic Pizza Toast 68
Garlic Tilapia 31

Printed in Great Britain
by Amazon

28487010R00066